"*Mindfulness for Bipolar Disorder* extends far beyond management of bipolar symptoms. This easy-to-read, well-written book is a valuable resource for all humans, whether living with bipolar disorder, another chronic illness, or life in general (which can be a chronic condition). The practice of mindfulness is a gift, available to all, that will have a powerful impact on your life."

> —**Karen Dittrich, MD**, discovered mindfulness
> and meditation after being diagnosed with
> multiple sclerosis twenty-two years ago

"[Marchand's] book is a breakthrough in the advancement of the treatment of bipolar disorder, as a more intractable condition. In this book, readers will find a combination of scientific knowledge and the techniques of meditation as practiced for centuries. As a highly regarded psychiatrist, Marchand is able to offer proven methods for the cessation of suffering. By doing so, he has shown not only his professional acumen, but also his compassionate heart and wisdom in the service of others."

> —**Victor Perri**, practicing Zen Buddhist
> and lawyer for over thirty years in areas
> including labor, employment, disability
> law, and civil rights

"In *Mindfulness for Bipolar Disorder*, Marchand offers a unique flavor of mindfulness practice for a serious and difficult mental illness. It combines well-balanced, ancient, traditional techniques with modern empirical, practical, and repeatable wisdom from Western science and medicine. *Mindfulness for Bipolar Disorder* covers a remarkably broad range of symptoms of the illness—including the quite nuanced, such as noticing the difference between 'pleasure' and 'happiness'—with pragmatic tools and techniques for their management. Marchand's style of writing is not only accessible and easy to understand but is also influenced by deep kindness and compassion for his patients. Readers can expect to have the sense that their condition is not a hopeless and untenable disorder, but rather a challenging set of symptoms that can be managed with relatively simple mindfulness-based practices."

—**Adam Shishin Lintz**, husband, father, student
  of and practitioner in the Soto Zen tradition,
  software architect, and martial artist

"Marchand's caring professionalism comes through in spades in his insightful and compassionately written book, *Mindfulness for Bipolar Disorder*. With a clear understanding of the science behind both bipolar disorder and mindfulness practice, Marchand honors readers' unique struggles, while encouraging hope for a better future. If you buy one book on bipolar disorder, make it this one."

—**Erica Marken**, Soto Zen Buddhist who serves
  on the board of directors for Two Arrows Zen
  Center in Salt Lake City, UT

mindfulness
for bipolar disorder

HOW MINDFULNESS *and* NEUROSCIENCE CAN HELP YOU MANAGE YOUR BIPOLAR SYMPTOMS

William R. Marchand, MD

New Harbinger Publications, Inc.

Publisher's Note

This publication is designed to provide accurate and authoritative information in regard to the subject matter covered. It is sold with the understanding that the publisher is not engaged in rendering psychological, financial, legal, or other professional services. If expert assistance or counseling is needed, the services of a competent professional should be sought.

Distributed in Canada by Raincoast Books

Copyright © 2015 by William R. Marchand
New Harbinger Publications, Inc.
5674 Shattuck Avenue
Oakland, CA 94609
www.newharbinger.com

Cover design by Amy Shoup
Acquired by Melissa Kirk
Edited by Brady Kahn

Library of Congress Cataloging-in-Publication Data on file

Printed in the United States of America

17	16	15								

| 10 | 9 | 8 | 7 | 6 | 5 | 4 | 3 | 2 | 1 | First printing |

Contents

Part 2
Your Mindfulness Plan for Solving the Bipolar Puzzle

introduction

This book is for anyone who suffers from bipolar disorder. As you know, this illness can be very difficult to treat. Traditional treatments, such as medication and psychotherapy, are effective; however, many people continue to experience depression, mood elevations, and other symptoms despite receiving appropriate care. Unfortunately, very few people with bipolar disorder are completely symptom-free as a result of conventional treatments alone. That is the bipolar puzzle—how to live well with a chronic condition that doesn't always respond well to treatment.

To live with your illness, it is critical for you to use as many recovery strategies as possible. The aim of this book is to provide another effective tool for your bipolar recovery toolbox. That tool is mindfulness meditation.

A Mindful Approach to Bipolar Symptoms

Are you ready to try a new approach to living with bipolar disorder? The mindful approach to bipolar symptoms is radically different from traditional treatments. By practicing meditation, you can learn how to be present with your bipolar symptoms rather than try to get rid of them. Doing this will, in turn, make your symptoms less intense. This may seem counterintuitive, but it works. Our minds normally respond to symptoms with automatic thinking patterns that actually make them worse. In contrast, unpleasant emotional states tend to become less intense and fade away when we let them be. Learning how to do this can totally change your relationship with your illness. Mindfulness isn't about being passive, though. Once you see and experience reality as it is through mindful awareness, you have the freedom to act. Mindfulness is about liberating yourself from habitual thinking patterns and behaviors that keep you stuck.

Scientific research has shown that mindfulness is helpful for people with bipolar disorder and that meditation practice can rewire the bipolar brain. In this book, I will guide you through the process of developing a mindfulness meditation practice that will help you live well with bipolar disorder.

The idea for this book originated with my own practice of mindfulness in the Soto Zen Buddhist tradition. In this tradition, we aim to sit in open awareness, watching phenomena arise and pass. By doing so, we see that everything is impermanent, including our own thoughts and emotions. Like clouds in the sky, they arise and pass. We also see that our minds tend to cling to certain things, often negative experiences and feelings. Through awareness of the present moment, we can notice our tendency to hold on to negativity and we can let it go. We can relax in the moment without needing to fix or change anything. That ability has helped me to fully appreciate my own life, moment by moment.

The Zen tradition also has a strong emphasis on compassion, and while there are many ways to practice compassion, we focus on sharing the transformative power of mindfulness with others. This ties in with my work as a psychiatrist, where over many years of working with bipolar patients, I've recognized the need for more creative tools to reduce their suffering. That recognition led me to start teaching mindfulness classes for people with bipolar disorder—and now it has led to this book.

Writing this book is an extension of my work as a mindfulness teacher and my personal mindfulness practice. Articulating the concepts of mindfulness to help you solve the bipolar puzzle has deepened my own understanding and practice.

What Is Mindfulness Meditation?

Meditation can sound mysterious, but it is simply the process of focusing your attention rather than letting your mind wander. You can be mindful at any time or in any place. For example, during daily life, you can focus all of your attention on any activity, such as washing your hair or taking out the garbage. During formal meditation, the focus can be on the breath or on physical sensations. The aim is to be fully present in each moment, feeling the sensations, hearing the sounds, and seeing the sights. This sounds simple—and it is a very simple concept—but it is a skill each of us has to learn. Our minds don't want to stay focused on one topic. They tend to wander and ruminate.

Try this simple experiment. Sit in a comfortable position and close your eyes. Start counting your breaths. Count "one" for the first inhalation-exhalation cycle, "two" for the next cycle, and so on. Count to ten and then start over. Do this for about three minutes. If your attention wanders and you lose count, then start over with one. Notice what happens. For most people, the mind immediately starts to drift. We start to think about the past or the future rather than stay focused on the breath. Sometimes we may not be able to count beyond two or three before the mind meanders down some path or other.

In mindfulness language, this tendency of the mind to wander is referred to as *autopilot*, because the mind automatically starts to think about the past or the future. Most of the time, you don't make a conscious decision to think about something; your mind goes there on its own. Autopilot isn't good or bad; it's just how the mind works. However, many of these automatic thinking patterns can be less than helpful. An example that may be familiar to you is having repetitive thoughts that are excessively self-critical. Another unhelpful thinking pattern is spending hours turning something over and over in your mind when you are upset. You can be carried away by these thoughts without even realizing it.

Autopilot thinking patterns are often associated with unpleasant emotions, such as sadness, anger, or anxiety. Most importantly, these patterns have been shown to intensify mood symptoms and to contribute to anxiety, stress, and depression. The good news is that there is a solution for the problem of autopilot. It is called mindfulness meditation. That is what this book is about.

Mindfulness is a type of meditation during which you focus your attention on the present moment. As best you can, you keep your awareness on the sights, sounds, and physical sensations that are occurring right now—in this very moment. This is in contrast to autopilot, which is always fixated on the past or future. When practicing mindfulness, you experience thoughts and emotions, but instead of being carried away by the never-ending torrent of cognitions and feelings that can flood your mind, you experience your thoughts and emotions as an observer. By developing a mindfulness practice, you can spend more time with your attention in the present moment, just watching the deluge.

Mindfulness Meditation Practice for Bipolar Disorder

Living our lives more mindfully has many benefits. This is true for everyone, but a mindfulness practice can be especially helpful for the symptoms of bipolar disorder.

As you know, bipolar disorder causes episodes of both depression and mania. Symptoms of depressed mood include sadness, the inability to experience pleasure, negative thinking, and disturbances of sleep and appetite. In contrast, mania involves excessively happy or irritable moods, high energy, rapid speech, and out-of-character behaviors. Those with bipolar disorder often also experience anxiety (an excessive or inappropriate fear response), irritability, and negative thinking. Bipolar disorder also can cause unreasonable beliefs about the self. Finally, because of bipolar disorder, you may find it difficult to experience joy and satisfaction in your life. A mindfulness meditation practice can help you manage these symptoms and be happier.

Your Eight-Step Mindfulness Recovery Plan

This book provides an eight-step mindfulness recovery plan to help you manage the symptoms of bipolar disorder and lead a more joyful and satisfying life. Part 1 explains how mindfulness can help you. Part 2 of this book provides the steps you can take to develop your own mindfulness practice. Here is a preview.

Step 1: Your Daily Meditation Practice

Sitting meditation is the foundation of a mindfulness practice. In chapter 4, you will start your bipolar recovery plan by learning how to practice sitting meditation on a daily basis.

Step 2: Targeting Bipolar Depression

Autopilot thinking patterns often bring on or worsen bipolar depression. Sometimes negative thinking patterns lead to feelings of depression, or it can be the other way around: feeling sad can bring on autopilot. Either way, autopilot thinking patterns and symptoms of depression almost always end up in a vicious cycle with each making the other worse. The solution is to move into a mental state of mindful awareness of the present moment. In chapter 5, you will learn to use a short meditation, the mindful minute, to move out of autopilot and into mindfulness when you are feeling depressed.

Step 3: Calming the Anxiety of Bipolar Disorder

You experience anxiety when your fear response is malfunctioning. Either you feel anxious for no reason (an out-of-the-blue attack of panic) or your response to a given situation is greater than the situation deserves (you may experience excessive worry and anxiety in response to stress). The brain's autopilot thinking response to anxiety almost always makes it worse. Chapter 6 will teach you to sit in meditation with anxiety and let it fade away.

Step 4: Observing Your Thinking Patterns

People with bipolar disorder tend to think negatively about life in general and about themselves in particular, and these automatic thinking patterns can increase depression and anxiety. In chapter 7, you will learn to become more skillful at being a mindful observer of your negative thoughts about life and yourself. In meditation, you can stay in the moment and watch your thoughts come and go like clouds in the sky. As you watch your thoughts, you can see how they are often irrational and illogical. Watching them gives you distance from them.

Step 5: Working with Bipolar Mania and Desire

One of the most troublesome symptoms of mania is intense desire. This can lead to out-of-character behaviors, such as excessive shopping, substance use, and sexual promiscuity. Chapter 8 builds upon previous chapters and extends your mindfulness practice to being present with desire. Rather than feel the need to act on cravings, you can learn how to watch these feelings as they come and go. However, getting to this point takes considerable practice.

Step 6: Managing Irritability and Anger

Irritability and anger are common symptoms of bipolar disorder and can occur during either depression or mania. Of course, feeling frustrated and upset from time to time is normal, but as with excessive desire, too much irritability can cause problems in your life. In chapter 9, you will learn to use mindfulness to manage anger and irritability.

Step 7: Rethinking Your Bipolar Self

You may be overly self-critical during depression and have an inflated sense of self during mania. Chapter 10 will help you develop a new relationship with your thoughts about yourself. You will discover through mindful awareness that you are perfect in each moment and that there is nothing that you need to fix or change.

Step 8: Being Bipolar and Happy

Autopilot thinking can mislead you into believing that happiness is based upon external circumstances—that you'll be happy when you get this or that (new car, new phone), when something or other happens (you get a raise at work, go on vacation), or maybe when you get rid of something that you have but don't want (a debt, a conflict with your partner). Mindfulness teaches you that the mind is never satisfied. Nothing you can get (or get rid of) will make you happy. Chapter 11 will show you how true joy and happiness exist in each and every moment—right now—rather than at some point in the future. By learning to stay in the present moment, you become able to see and experience the joy that was there all along.

How to Use This Book

The chapters in this book are meant to build on each other, so you should read them in order, starting with chapter 1. Part 1 helps you prepare for the mindfulness practices that you'll begin in part 2. Chapter 1 explains how mindfulness can help those with bipolar disorder and includes a review of the evidence for the effectiveness of mindfulness-based interventions. Chapter 2 covers the neuroscience underlying bipolar disorder and underlying mindfulness. Chapter 3 covers some basic concepts of mindfulness meditation, including the need for self-compassion.

In part 2, it's important to do all the meditation exercises, practicing them as well as you can. An appendix provides some other meditations that you may want to try. In addition, you may find guided meditations to be helpful, especially as you first start to practice mindfulness. Therefore, guided audio versions of all the meditations in part 2—and of two meditations in the appendix—are available for you to download at http://www.newharbinger.com/31854. (See the very end of this book for more information.)

This book is based on my experience teaching mindfulness to individuals with bipolar disorder as well as on my personal meditation practice. In most chapters, you'll find stories about real people with bipolar disorder who are using mindfulness to live well with it. These stories come from my work as a psychiatrist and mindfulness teacher, and I hope you'll find them inspiring as well as instructive. The stories are all true, but details have been extensively changed so that no story represents an actual person.

This book is also based upon research. A reference list at the end includes all the cited sources, which you can use for further information on any given topic. I've also included a list of suggested reading material and a glossary of important terms.

You may have already taken or be planning to take an in-person mindfulness class. If so, this book will complement what you learn. Taking a class is a great idea, but you also can use this book without a class. It will provide you with everything you need to develop a mindfulness practice. You also may want to consider joining fellow mindfulness practitioners online for support and information at http://www.WilliamRMarchandMD.com.

What You Can Expect

Mindfulness is a powerful tool. However, it is important to have realistic expectations about it. Your meditation practice won't cure bipolar disorder or keep you from ever having episodes of depression or mania. However, with mindfulness you can expect to have fewer episodes and you can expect the episodes that you do have to be less severe. By spending more time in mindful awareness and less time on autopilot, you also can experience more joy in your life.

This book and your mindfulness meditation practice are not intended to replace any of your other treatments, though your meditation practice may help your other treatments work better. In particular, mindfulness meditation can help you get more from psychotherapy. This is because psychotherapy is about change. In order to change, it is necessary to first become fully aware of your own autopilot-driven thinking patterns and behaviors. Mindfulness helps you see these clearly in the moment as they occur. Importantly, you learn to observe these patterns and behaviors without self-judgment. Nonjudgmental awareness of how our minds work is the key to change.

Without exception, everyone who has completed one of my mindfulness classes has found it to be helpful. Many have found it to be life changing. But while mindfulness is a deceptively simple concept, being mindful is harder than it looks. It is a skill that anyone can learn, but it takes practice. What does this mean for you? If you want to add this tool to your recovery toolbox, it means practicing the methods in this book. You will have to practice meditation almost every day. Daily practice is best. That said, none of us ever practices as much as we want to. Just do the best you can and always have compassion for yourself.

Mindfulness is experiential. Reading this book is like reading a menu. Practicing meditation is like eating the meal. I am honored to take this nourishment with you. Let's get started.

part 1

---

getting ready to practice

chapter 1

---

the missing piece in the bipolar puzzle

This chapter discusses how and why a mindfulness practice can help you live better with bipolar disorder. It opens with a brief review of the language of bipolar disorder. Before getting started, however, I want to acknowledge that you know more about bipolar disorder than I ever will. You live with it every day. My purpose is not to tell you all about bipolar disorder but rather to make sure that we are speaking the same language. Bipolar terminology can be complex and confusing, so this is a good place to begin.

Talking About Bipolar Disorder

You may have been diagnosed with a subtype of bipolar disorder. There are three primary diagnostic subtypes: bipolar I disorder, bipolar II disorder, and cyclothymic disorder (American Psychiatric Association 2013). There are additional diagnostic categories for bipolar symptoms that are due to another medical condition as well as other categories for bipolar symptoms that do not meet all of the diagnostic criteria for one of the three primary subtypes. Because there is more than one bipolar condition, the term *spectrum* is commonly used to refer to the entire group of bipolar disorders. The information provided in this book is for anyone with bipolar disorder, regardless of the specific type, and the words "bipolar disorder" and "bipolar spectrum" will be used interchangeably.

Bipolar Mood Episodes

Bipolar spectrum conditions are mood disorders. People with bipolar disorder experience two kinds of mood abnormalities: major depressive episodes and periods of mood elevations. In other words, people with bipolar disorder experience both poles of the mood spectrum. That's where the term *bipolar* comes from. Table 1.1 lists the symptoms required for a diagnosis of a bipolar depressive episode. Episodes of mood elevations are called *manic episodes*, if severe, or *hypomanic episodes*, if milder. Table 1.2 lists the symptoms required for a diagnosis of a manic episode, and table 1.3 lists the symptoms required for a diagnosis of a hypomanic episode.

Table 1.1
Diagnostic Criteria for a Bipolar Depressive Episode

Five or more of the following symptoms must have been present for at least two weeks and include either depressed mood or loss of interest and pleasure; these symptoms must occur most of the day, nearly every day, and cause significant distress or impairment:

- Depressed mood

- Markedly diminished interest or pleasure in most activities

- Increased or decreased weight or appetite

- Increased sleep or insomnia

- Increased or decreased motor activity

- Fatigue or loss of energy

- Feelings of worthlessness or excessive or inappropriate guilt

- Diminished ability to think or concentrate, or indecisiveness

- Recurrent thoughts of death or suicide (American Psychiatric Association 2013)

Table 1.2
Diagnostic Criteria for a Manic Episode

A manic episode is a period of abnormally elevated or irritable mood along with increased activity, lasting at least one week (or any duration if symptoms are so serious that hospitalization is required). Psychotic symptoms may be present. Manic symptoms are present most of the day, nearly every day, and interfere with your ability to function. They must include three or more of the following symptoms—or four or more of these symptoms if your mood is irritable but not abnormally elevated—that represent a noticeable change from your usual behavior:

- Inflated self-esteem or grandiosity

- Decreased need for sleep

- More talkative, or feeling pressure to keep talking

- Thoughts going faster than normal

- Distractibility

- Increased goal-directed activity

- Excessive involvement in pleasurable activities that have a high potential for painful consequences, such as buying sprees or sexual indiscretions (American Psychiatric Association 2013)

Table 1.3
Diagnostic Criteria for a Hypomanic Episode

A hypomanic episode is a period lasting at least four days of abnormally elevated or irritable mood along with increased activity, with symptoms present most of the day, nearly every day. Symptoms do not limit your ability to function, require hospitalization, or include psychosis, but they represent a clear change in behavior from normal and are obvious to friends and family.

They must include three or more of the following symptoms—or four or more if your mood is irritable but not abnormally elevated—that represent a noticeable change from your usual behavior:

- Inflated self-esteem or grandiosity

- Decreased need for sleep

- More talkative, or feeling pressure to keep talking

- Thoughts going faster than normal

- Distractibility

- Increased goal-directed activity

- Excessive involvement in pleasurable activities that have a high potential for painful consequences, such as buying sprees or sexual indiscretions (American Psychiatric Association 2013)

Bipolar Subtypes

For a diagnosis of bipolar I disorder, you must have had at least one manic episode. Almost everyone diagnosed with bipolar I disorder also experiences depressive episodes and hypomanic episodes, and many people with bipolar I disorder often experience even milder mood elevations as well. In this book, *mood elevations* is a general term referring to episodes of manic or hypomanic symptoms, as well as to episodes that are even milder.

A diagnosis of bipolar II disorder requires at least one episode of major depression and at least one hypomanic episode, but manic episodes are not part of the picture. If you were diagnosed with bipolar II disorder and then experienced a manic episode, your diagnosis would change to bipolar I.

Cyclothymic disorder is when there are episodes of mood elevations that do not meet the full criteria for a hypomanic or a manic episode, and there are periods of depression that do not meet the full criteria for a major depressive episode. Additionally, to meet the diagnostic criteria for cyclothymic disorder, the mood episodes must be numerous over a two-year period for adults or over one year for children and adolescents. Table 1.4 lists the diagnostic criteria for major depressive disorder, bipolar I disorder, bipolar II disorder, and cyclothymic disorder.

Table 1.4
Diagnostic Criteria for Mood Disorders

Disorder	Required	May also have	May not have
Major depressive disorder	Major depressive episode	Mild depressive episodes	Manic or hypomanic episodes
Bipolar I disorder	Manic episode	Depression and hypomania	N/A
Bipolar II disorder	Major depression and hypomania	Mild depressive episodes	Manic episodes
Cyclothymic disorder	Mild episodes of depression and mood elevations	N/A	Major depressive, manic, or hypomanic episodes

(American Psychiatric Association 2013)

Bipolar Disorder over Time

Bipolar disorder is considered a chronic condition. Chronic means that it is long lasting. Many other medical conditions are chronic, such as diabetes, high blood pressure, and heart disease. Like most other chronic conditions, bipolar disorder is considered a lifelong illness. Once someone gets this condition, it does not go away on its own, and it requires long-term treatment. Unfortunately, there is currently no cure for bipolar disorder. Therefore, the aim of treatment is remission of symptoms. In other words, the goal is to get rid of any current mood symptoms and then to prevent relapse.

This chapter will describe conventional treatments for bipolar disorder and then introduce the benefits of adding a mindfulness practice to your treatment program, as a client named Eve did. Her story will help to illustrate the challenges of diagnosing and treating bipolar disorder.

• Eve's Story

Eve has bipolar II disorder. Her first episode, at age seventeen, was a major depressive episode. This episode was severe and caused significant impairment. Before becoming depressed, she had been an honors student and a star player on her high school volleyball team. Once she became depressed, her grades suffered, and she quit the volleyball team. She no longer had much energy or motivation to do anything, she slept too much, she lost her ability to experience pleasure, and her mood was profoundly low. She ultimately attempted suicide and was subsequently hospitalized.

Eve's depression was rapidly followed by several hypomanic episodes, and she was diagnosed with bipolar II when she was eighteen. Since then, Eve has never had a mood elevation that meets the criteria for a manic episode, which is why her diagnosis has remained bipolar II. Eve also has milder mood episodes, which could give the appearance of cyclothymic disorder. The difference is that Eve has had at least one episode that meets the criteria for a full mood episode.

Today, Eve is forty and experiences very good control of her symptoms. She has only short mild episodes of depression and has not had a mood elevation for several years. Her depressive episodes usually last a few days at most and come on only every few months. However, this was not always true. Like many people with bipolar illness, Eve did not respond to the first medications that she tried. Over the first few years of her treatment, she continued to have severe episodes of major depression that would last a month or more, and she also had several hypomanic episodes each year. For Eve, the difficulty was finding a treatment approach that was effective at preventing relapse. What eventually worked for her was taking a mood stabilizer to control her current symptoms, and using psychotherapy as well as mindfulness to help prevent depressive episodes. Fortunately, Eve and her mental health care providers were eventually able to find this combination of medication and nonmedical treatments, which has helped Eve reach a place where she can live well with her disorder.

Eve's experience of bipolar disorder is not unusual. Diagnosis as well as treatment can be a challenge. It may take time and some experimentation in treatment to find out what works best.

Conventional Treatments for Bipolar Disorder

Bipolar spectrum disorders are conventionally treated with medications and psychotherapy. For bipolar I disorder, medication is considered to be required. Those with bipolar II disorder also typically require medication as a component of their treatment. There is less research available to guide the treatment of cyclothymic disorder.

Medication Treatment of Bipolar Spectrum Symptoms

Bipolar disorder frequently requires the use of more than one medication, which is sometimes called *combination therapy*—as opposed to *monotherapy*, when only one medication is needed.

Three categories of medications are effective for the treatment of mania or hypomania: anticonvulsants, lithium, and antipsychotics (Goodwin 2009). These medications are often called *mood stabilizers.* Anticonvulsants were originally developed to treat epilepsy, but two of these, valproate and carbamazepine, are effective for mania. There are two general categories of antipsychotics, first-generation agents and second-generation agents (SGAs). While both are effective for mood elevations, only SGAs are typically used in the United States to treat bipolar disorder.

For someone with severe manic symptoms, treatment might start with lithium, valproate, or an SGA. An SGA is typically used if psychotic symptoms (hallucinations or delusions) are present. There is some evidence that combining SGAs with other mood stabilizers is the most effective treatment for mania (Scherk, Pajonk, and Leucht 2007), so two medications may be used for severe symptoms or if there is an incomplete response to one medication. For milder mania, monotherapy is more common.

Bipolar depression is treated differently from unipolar depression. Antidepressants are the primary treatment for unipolar depression, whereas some research suggests that using antidepressants alone for bipolar depression can bring on mood elevations or cause more frequent shifts, or *cycling,* between mania and depression (Vazquez, Tondo, and Baldessarini 2011; Pacchiarotti et al. 2011). Because of this, most experts recommend against treating bipolar depression with antidepressants alone. Some research suggests that antidepressants can be safely used in combination with a mood stabilizer, but the effectiveness of antidepressants for bipolar depression has been questioned (Nivoli et al. 2011), and many experts recommend mood stabilizers as the primary treatment (Grunze et al. 2010; Yatham et al. 2009).

Finding the right medication often takes time. For example, Eve was initially treated with antidepressants alone and then continued on antidepressants in combination with a mood stabilizer. In retrospect, it seems likely that antidepressants were causing her to cycle and have frequent relapses.

Psychotherapy for Bipolar Disorder

Psychological approaches to bipolar treatment play an important role, and research indicates that adding psychotherapy to medication enhances the symptomatic and functional outcomes of bipolar disorder (Miklowitz 2008). Interpersonal and social rhythm therapy, cognitive therapy, interpersonal therapy, and family-focused therapy have all been recommended as adjunctive treatments for depression; however, there is currently no evidence to suggest that any psychotherapy strategy is effective for mania (Goodwin 2009). Further, many people experiencing mania (unless it's very mild) will most likely be unable to participate in psychotherapy. Cognitive therapy is one of the most commonly used psychotherapies for depression, and its aim is to change thinking patterns that are illogical and unhelpful.

A mindfulness practice can help you achieve benefits from cognitive therapy as well as other psychotherapies. Eve found that her mindfulness practice helped her recognize some thinking patterns that had become a habit for her and were making her symptoms worse. Since mindfulness facilitates uncritical acceptance, she was able to recognize these autopilot thinking patterns and to avoid being critical of herself for having them.

The bottom line is that while effective conventional treatments are available, the treatment of bipolar spectrum disorders is challenging. In particular, bipolar depression often does not respond well to treatment (Sienaert et al. 2013). Traditional psychiatric medication and psychotherapy approaches are not enough. That's where a mindfulness practice can come in. While practicing mindfulness cannot replace any of these treatments, it can help.

Mindfulness and Meditation for Bipolar Disorder

Developing a mindfulness meditation practice takes time and effort, but it is time and effort well spent. A number of investigations have looked specifically at whether mindfulness may be helpful for those with bipolar disorder. The answer is yes, it can. One study indicated that mindfulness could be used effectively by individuals with bipolar spectrum illness (Weber et al. 2010). Other studies have shown improvement in depression (Deckersbach et al. 2012), anxiety (Perich et al. 2013), and emotional regulation and thinking ability (Ives-Deliperi et al. 2013; Deckersbach et al. 2012).

Mindfulness also can help reduce negative mood states, help you to relate differently to negative thoughts, and reduce the impact of mood episodes (Chadwick et al. 2011). Finally, there is evidence for increased psychological well-being, positive mood, and psychosocial functioning (Deckersbach et al. 2012).

Many studies of other conditions also show that mindfulness is helpful for the symptoms of bipolar disorder. Much of this research involves two mindfulness-based programs that were developed for clinical use. The first of these, mindfulness-based stress reduction (MBSR), was developed by Dr. Jon Kabat-Zinn (2013) at the University of Massachusetts Medical Center as a secular method to utilize Buddhist mindfulness meditation in mainstream clinical practice. MBSR includes education about stress and ways to cope with it. The mindfulness component includes sitting meditation, a body scan (sequentially focusing on sensations of specific body parts), and yoga. MBSR also involves the cultivation of a number of attitudes, including becoming an impartial witness to your own experience, acceptance of things as they actually are in the present moment, and watching your thoughts come and go (Kabat-Zinn 2013).

Mindfulness-based cognitive therapy (MBCT) was developed by Zindel Segal, Mark Williams, and John Teasdale (2002). MBCT is based upon MBSR and combines the principles of cognitive psychotherapy with those of mindfulness. MBCT also uses secular mindfulness techniques and teaches recognition of and disengagement from patterns of ruminative negative thinking that contribute to mood and anxiety symptoms. Some of what you will learn in this book is drawn from MBSR and MBCT.

How Mindfulness Can Help

You can reasonably expect that mindfulness will help you live with bipolar disorder. This book specifically targets these bipolar symptoms: depression, anxiety, negative thinking patterns, impulsive behaviors, irritability and anger, and poor self-concept. Here's some additional evidence for how it works.

Reducing Bipolar Depression

Depression typically causes much more distress than mania, so reducing depression can have a very positive impact on your life. (See table 1.1 for common symptoms of depression.) The mindfulness methods that you will learn in this book draw on those used in MBSR and MBCT but are modified here to address bipolar disorder. The evidence supporting this approach comes from studies indicating that MBCT, which was specifically developed for depression, can help reduce current symptoms (Van Aalderen et al. 2012) and prevent recurrence (Segal et al. 2010). There is also strong evidence that MBSR works for depression (Goldin and Gross 2010). Chapter 5 uses mindfulness techniques to specifically target bipolar depression.

Managing Anxiety

Most people with bipolar disorder experience anxiety. Many studies have shown that mindfulness can reduce anxiety (Vollestad, Sivertsen, and Nielsen 2011). Chapter 6 will teach you how to use mindfulness to manage your anxiety.

Addressing Bipolar Thinking Patterns

Chapter 7 tackles the problem of ruminative thinking, which contributes to depression, anxiety, irritability, and low self-esteem. A number of studies have shown that a mindfulness practice leads to less ruminative thinking (Campbell et al. 2012).

Checking Impulsive Behaviors

Mania and hypomania (see tables 1.2 and 1.3) may cause an intense desire for pleasurable activities and lead to impulsive behaviors, such as spending sprees, substance use, and sexual indiscretions, without regard for the consequences of your actions. Chapter 8 will help you use mindfulness to be present with desire without needing to take action to satisfy it.

Decreasing Irritability and Anger

Excessive irritability is a common bipolar symptom associated with both depression and mania. Mindfulness has been shown to reduce emotional reactivity (Goldin and Gross 2010) and thus decrease the tendency to respond to situations with intense anger. Chapter 9 will show you how to experience less irritability.

Improving Your Self-Concept

Chapter 10 targets how you think about yourself. Most people with bipolar disorder have self-critical and self-deprecating thinking patterns. You will learn how to break out of this thinking rut and realize that, in each moment, you are perfect just as you are.

Finding Happiness and Joy

Mindfulness is also about finding happiness and joy in being bipolar. You can expect to do this too. The final chapter of this book is dedicated to helping you discover the delight of being fully present with your life, moment by moment and breath by breath.

Like many people with bipolar disorder, you may believe that it's impossible to experience true happiness. Through mindfulness, however, you will come to see how limiting that belief is; you will discover that it just isn't true. Of course, bipolar disorder isn't easy to live with, but you can experience as much enjoyment and pleasure in your life as anyone else.

What's Next?

Chapter 2 will discuss the neuroscience of bipolar disorder and show how you can use mindfulness to rewire your brain. Chapter 3 will provide everything you need to know about the practice of mindfulness and meditation. With that background, you can start on your eight-step mindfulness recovery plan, which is covered in part 2.

how mindfulness can rewire your brain

This chapter is about the science of bipolar disorder and the science of mindfulness. First it covers some general information about genetics and bipolar disorder. Then it goes into how the human brain works and talks about what isn't working right when you have bipolar disorder. Finally, it shows how mindfulness can rewire your bipolar brain circuitry.

You might be wondering if taking in all this new information is necessary. Can mindfulness help you manage your illness even if you don't know how it works? You can certainly practice mindfulness without fully understanding it. Having some knowledge of the science involved can be beneficial, however. It was for Eve, whom you met in chapter 1. Eve, who describes herself as a skeptical person, found it reassuring to know that there is a scientific basis for how mindfulness works. That knowledge helped her make the commitment to develop a consistent mindfulness practice. Hopefully, understanding the science behind mindfulness will help you make that same commitment.

Genetics and Bipolar Disorder

Before discussing the brain, it's important to briefly mention genetics, because genetic (or inherited) abnormalities cause most of the brain changes that underlie bipolar symptoms. Many studies have demonstrated that bipolar and other mood disorders are partly caused by genetic factors. The word "partly" is important here, for the evidence indicates that what is inherited is not the actual illness but a *vulnerability*, or risk, for developing the illness. That is, you would have a greater vulnerability for bipolar disorder if a close relative has or had bipolar disorder. Eve's maternal grandmother and mother both had bipolar disorder, so she inherited a very significant risk for having the illness. In most cases, it is a combination of genetic and environmental factors that actually determines whether you develop bipolar disorder. Genetic factors cause most of the disruptions of brain circuitry in bipolar disorder, but environmental influences, such as stress, lifestyle factors, and damage to the brain from substances or injury, also may disturb brain circuit function.

Some Brain Basics

To understand bipolar disorder and how mindfulness can help you, you need to know a little bit about how the human brain works. Like a computer or smartphone, the brain has a number of components, or regions, that perform specific functions and are connected by wiring, or neurons. Brain regions that are connected to each other are called *neural circuits*. Problems with these circuits play a role in bipolar disorder, so it's important for you to understand how this circuitry works. The next section goes into more detail.

Neurons and Neurotransmitters

Neurons, or nerve cells, are the brain's wiring. Their task is to transmit information from one place to another in the nervous system. All neurons have similar structures; they are long, skinny cells with distinct regions, known as the *dendrites, cell body,* and *axon* (see figure 2.1). The dendrites receive information, and the axon is where information travels to another neuron. The cell body is the neuron's control center.

Information is transmitted as a message along individual nerve cells by way of an electrical impulse. When the impulse reaches the end of the nerve cell, the information needs to pass to one or more other neurons to form a circuit. Information passes from one neuron to another by way of a specialized structure called the *synapse.* This is where the axon of one neuron forms a connection with the dendrite of another nerve cell. However, there is a slight gap between the two connecting nerves, which is called the *synaptic cleft.* Information is passed across this gap by way of chemicals called *neurotransmitters.*

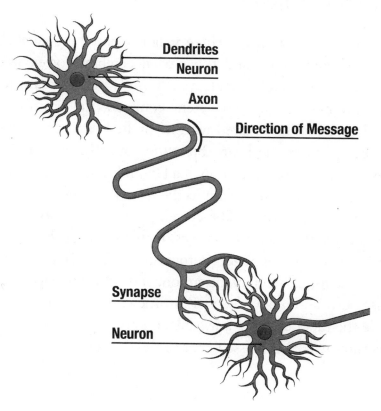

Figure 2.1: Neuron and Synapse

Several neurotransmitters are thought to play an important role in the causes of bipolar disorder. These include serotonin, norepinephrine, dopamine, glutamate, and gamma-aminobutyric acid (GABA). Medications used to treat bipolar disorder are thought to work, at least in part, by modifying neurotransmitter function.

Brain Structure

The human brain has three major regions: the cerebellum, the brain stem, and the medial cerebral cortex (see figure 2.2). The cerebellum plays a key role in motor control and movement. The brain stem connects the brain and spinal cord and is involved with many functions, including the regulation of the heart, breathing, and the sleep cycle. The medial cortex is made up of a left and right hemisphere. Each hemisphere is divided into the frontal, parietal, temporal, and occipital lobes. The cortex processes sensory information, initiates motor behaviors, regulates emotion, and is the center of the higher-brain functions, often called *executive functions*, of memory, attention, thought, language, and consciousness. Finally, deep within the cortex, and below it, reside the hippocampus, amygdala, and basal ganglia. These structures will be discussed later in the chapter.

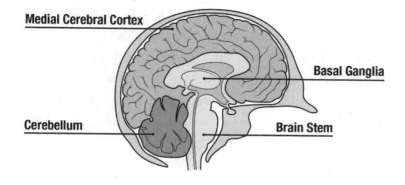

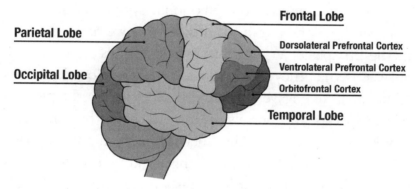

Figure 2.2: Human Brain Anatomy

Brain Function and Bipolar Symptoms

The symptoms of bipolar disorder are caused by disruptions of neurotransmitters and brain circuitry. Problems with brain circuitry result in both the emotional symptoms of bipolar disorder—depression, mania, anxiety, and irritability—and the *cognitive* (or thinking) symptoms, including the negative thinking of depression, the worry of anxiety, irrational thoughts about the self, and the tendency to ruminate, or to turn things over and over in the mind. A closer look at what happens when this circuitry is disrupted will help you understand both bipolar symptoms and the effects of mindfulness.

Emotional Symptoms

Before focusing on the emotional symptoms of bipolar disorder, it will be useful to consider why we have emotions in the first place. What do feelings do for us anyway? One answer is that they motivate us to take action. Emotions stimulate us to engage in behaviors necessary for the survival of our species and ourselves. Some feelings that are commonly thought of as negative, such as fear, anxiety, and anger, can motivate us to be alert for danger and to react to it. This is the well-known fight-or-flight response. Feelings of sadness or depression after the loss of a loved one may stimulate us to care for other humans. Other emotions, such as desire, love, or satisfaction, have a more positive tone. Desire encourages us to eat and to reproduce. Love leads us to develop relationships. The emotional symptoms of bipolar disorder are actually normal emotions that are excessive or inappropriate to a given situation.

So, you can see that emotional responses encourage behaviors necessary for survival. However, as humans, we also have an exceptional capacity to reason. For example, we can figure out that we need to eat just by thinking. We understand that if we don't eat, we will starve. Unlike other animals, we don't need strong emotions to inspire us to survive. Nevertheless, emotions are produced unconsciously in the older parts of our brains beneath the cortex.

Scientists think that human emotional life is similar to what it was thousands of years ago, before we developed the thinking abilities that we have now. The result is that sometimes our emotional responses can be excessive and unhelpful. This is a key point for understanding how mindfulness works, both in general and, more specifically, for bipolar disorder. During mindful awareness, you begin to realize that your emotions and thoughts are often meaningless. You begin to see excessive or unhelpful emotions for what they are: the firing of neurons in an outdated region of the brain. This realization can lead to these feelings becoming less powerful and compelling.

Depression and Mania

Depression and mania, the primary symptoms of bipolar disorder, occur as a result of problems with the brain circuitry that controls both pleasure and reward. This circuitry motivates us to eat, reproduce, and engage with others. Depression is manifested by an inability to experience pleasure, low motivation, and excessive sadness. In depression, the pleasure-and-reward circuits are underproducing. In contrast, these circuits are overproducing in mania, with its excessively happy mood (though it can be irritable), *euphoria* (unwarranted optimism), and sometimes exaggerated desire to engage in pleasurable activities.

The emotions associated with pleasure and reward are generated at an unconscious level by subcortical structures and are regulated by the cortex. A structure known as the *striatum*, along with the cortico-basal ganglia circuitry, is thought to produce the emotions of pleasure and reward. The cortex, which is the thinking and planning part of the brain, regulates emotional responses. Three regions—the dorsolateral prefrontal cortex, the ventrolateral prefrontal cortex, and the orbitofrontal cortex—on the outside and lower surfaces of the frontal lobe play a significant role in emotional control (see figure 2.2).

Another area that plays a key role in emotional regulation is the medial cerebral cortex. A number of studies have demonstrated abnormalities of the medial cortex in bipolar disorder, and it is very likely that failure of this region to adequately regulate emotion is a cause of bipolar symptoms.

Anxiety

Many people with bipolar disorder have anxiety symptoms, which can take many forms. Anxiety means that the fear response occurs at times when it's not needed, or it is excessive when there is actually a valid reason to be afraid. For example, Eve's panic symptoms were the result of her fear response being triggered out of the blue, when there was no actual danger.

The fight-or-flight response, as the name suggests, prepares the body for action. In a panic attack, your body responds as if there were a real threat. The heart starts beating faster, your breathing rate increases, and you may start to shake and sweat. This feels very unpleasant and can be scary, because the body is giving the message that there is danger, but the thinking part of the brain can't figure out what's wrong, since it doesn't see any threat. This is typical of what happens in a panic attack, but why does it happen?

One possibility is a faulty amygdala setting. Located in the brain's temporal lobe (see figure 2.2), the amygdala turns on the fight-or-flight response automatically whenever you sense danger. It's a great system except when it doesn't work correctly. Panic attacks can happen when the amygdala becomes too sensitive and sends threat signals for no reason. It's like having the thermostat in your home set too high, so the furnace turns on before the house gets cold. In Eve's case, it helped to understand that her panic symptoms were most likely just a faulty amygdala setting. Before having that knowledge, she had a tendency to worry about what the panic might mean, and her worrying often made her attacks more likely to happen. With a faulty amygdala setting, the problem is an excessive production of emotion.

Panic attacks also can happen because of faulty emotional regulation. The brain has a control mechanism in the frontal lobe and medial cerebral cortex that normally can evaluate the fear response to determine whether or not it's appropriate. When this mechanism comes online, you can think about the threat and your response. If you determine that all is safe, you can turn the alarm system off. Since there are brain processes for both the production and the regulation of emotion, panic attacks like Eve's could be the result of either a faulty amygdala setting or a problem with her regulatory system. It's generally thought that both can contribute to panic symptoms.

Cognitive Symptoms

Cognitive symptoms of bipolar disorder include the negative thinking of depression, the worry of anxiety, irrational thoughts about the self, and the tendency to ruminate. All of these can be understood as an exaggeration of normal thinking patterns. For example, some degree of worry can be normal and helpful, but when worrying becomes excessive, it causes distress and is unhelpful. This excessive thinking was defined in chapter 1 as autopilot thinking. Almost all of the troublesome thinking of bipolar disorder involves excessive autopilot thinking about yourself.

Autopilot Thinking About Yourself

We all spend a considerable amount of time doing *self-referential thinking*, or thinking about ourselves. This type of thinking is neither good nor bad; it is just the way the brain works. Self-referential thinking can be very helpful. For example, we can consider how we thought, felt, and acted in the past, and we can learn from those experiences. We can ponder our goals for the future and make appropriate plans. Our ability to think about the past and the future is what separates us from animals. It also helps us survive.

Self-referential thinking can be very unhelpful, however, when it takes the form of autopilot thinking. To review, autopilot thinking is when thoughts, emotions, and behaviors occur automatically without our making a conscious choice to think, feel, or act a certain way. It is the opposite of mindfulness. As you develop mindful awareness, you will most likely notice that your mind wanders frequently on autopilot down a path to review the past or to think about the future. This happens to everyone. It's what the mind does. Often autopilot includes self-referential thinking, and this automatic self-referential thinking can be a problem. There is a lot of evidence that this kind of thinking plays an important role in the mood and anxiety symptoms of bipolar disorder.

How does automatic thinking about yourself play a role in bipolar depression and anxiety? Here's what happens. It can start with the physical sensation of depression. Eve describes this as "a sick feeling in the pit of my stomach." No one likes that feeling. In response to this experience of discomfort, the mind automatically tries to figure out how to get rid of it. In other words, you may start ruminating about yourself and depression. Maybe it goes something like this: *Oh no, here it goes again. I hate feeling this way. What brought it on? What should I do? I wonder how long it will last. I really wanted to enjoy the party tomorrow.*

Does that sound familiar? This autopilot response can be helpful if it leads to taking action that helps you feel better. Often though, the thinking just goes around and around in circles. The circles may expand into stories: *The last time I was depressed, it lasted for three weeks. I couldn't get to sleep until two in the morning almost every night. I wasn't hungry, but I couldn't stop eating.* And so on. By getting stuck in this self-referential thinking mode, the autopilot response actually makes the depression worse. As you are trapped in thinking about depression, you become immobile and cannot move out of depression. This autopilot cycle is illustrated in figure 2.3. Later chapters will look at this process in much more detail. For now, it's enough to say that the purpose of practicing mindfulness is to give yourself a way out of the autopilot thinking that makes the depression and anxiety of bipolar disorder worse.

Figure 2.3: The Autopilot Cycle

Autopilot and the Medial Cortex

The medial cortex is the part of the brain where autopilot thinking about the self happens. Again, this area is also involved with emotional regulation. Thus, disruptions of the medial cortex contribute to both emotional and cognitive symptoms of bipolar disorder.

The medial cortex is part of an important neural circuit known as the *default mode network*, because it becomes active by default when the brain isn't engaged in other tasks. This means that we are automatically programmed to think about ourselves when nothing else is going on. This is important, because it tells us that autopilot is just the way the brain normally works. Again, it is neither good nor bad. There is a tendency when practicing mindfulness to become frustrated with autopilot because it is so persistent. It may be helpful for you to remember that autopilot is just the brain doing its job.

Brain Function and Your Mindfulness Practice

There are two reasons why it's important for you to know about brain function. First, it helps you understand the bipolar brain and how mindfulness can rewire it; the next section discusses how your mindfulness practice can change brain function. Second, this new understanding helps you use mindfulness to manage your bipolar symptoms.

One important message from this chapter is that the cognitive and emotional symptoms of bipolar disorder occur because of problems with brain circuitry. These symptoms have nothing to do with you as a person; they are a result of faulty wiring. Another takeaway is that these symptoms occur automatically. These two facts are very important for your mindfulness practice.

In mindfulness, the aim is to stay in the present moment and avoid being carried away by autopilot thoughts and emotions. The way you do this is by becoming a moment-by-moment observer of your own mental processes. It's like watching a drama on TV rather than being a part of the drama. Knowing that the cognitive and emotional symptoms of bipolar disorder are just a product of faulty wiring can help you in your mindfulness practice. By seeing symptoms for what they are—the firing of incorrectly wired neurons—you will find it much easier to be an observer, rather than a participant. As an observer, you will be able to get some distance from your symptoms. It's like watching a flooding river. If you are too close, you may fall in and get carried away, but if you observe from a distance, there is no danger of falling in and being swept downstream. Your knowledge of the causes of bipolar symptoms will help you maintain a safe distance from them.

Neuroplasticity and Brain Imaging

In the past, scientists thought that the adult human brain was fixed and generally unchangeable. In fact, because of a capacity known as *neuroplasticity*, our brains change in response to experience. With neuroplasticity, our brains can rewire to compensate for injury or in response to specific training, such as mindfulness. As you practice mindfulness, the brain's neuroplasticity gives you the ability to change autopilot thinking patterns and habitual emotional responses. That's how practicing mindfulness can help you with your bipolar symptoms.

We don't understand everything about how mindfulness changes the brain. However, neuroimaging studies conducted in recent years reveal a lot about how mindfulness works. Many studies of mindfulness have used functional neuroimaging. This means investigating how the brain functions, as opposed to studying brain structure. To use a computer analogy, it's like software versus hardware. Doctors and scientists have been able to evaluate the hardware of the brain structure for many years using CT and MRI scans, and these methods have been very important in diagnosing brain injuries, tumors, or strokes. But structural imaging doesn't reveal much about brain function at the software level. It's like pulling the components out of your computer: you can see if a component is broken or not, but you can't tell just by looking at the outside if the software is working properly. In contrast, functional brain imaging gives more information about the brain at the software level, and using this imaging, you can see how mindfulness reprograms the brain's software.

The Mindful Brain

It turns out that mindfulness changes many of the brain areas that are not working correctly in bipolar disorder. Functional imaging studies have demonstrated changes in the medial cortex and default mode network as well as in the amygdala and the striatum. As discussed above, the default mode network is involved in cognitive symptoms of bipolar disorder while the amygdala and striatum play a key role in emotional symptoms, and the medial cortex plays a role in both.

In addition, structural imaging studies have demonstrated that mindfulness and meditation can actually change the structure of the brain. These studies have shown changes in those regions noted in the functional imaging investigations and have also shown changes in the hippocampus. The hippocampus, located in the temporal lobe of the brain, is important for memory and emotional control. For skeptics like Eve (and me), the evidence that mindfulness meditation can change the structure of the brain provides a very persuasive reason to practice it.

In addition to the general brain changes described above, mindfulness has a positive impact on three specific neural processes in the bipolar brain: attention management, autopilot thinking, and emotional regulation.

Training Your Attention

Meditation is simply training your attention. To put it another way, when you meditate, you are training your mind to keep your attention focused where you want it. In mindfulness, this focus is on the physical sensations, sights, sounds, thoughts, and emotions occurring in the present moment. When your mind wanders off on autopilot, you gently direct your attention back to the present.

Scientists think that there are several networks in the brain that manage your attention. These networks involve the medial cortex and the basal ganglia (regions which are important for bipolar disorder) as well as other areas. Mindfulness appears to rewire these regions so that it is easier to keep your attention focused on the present moment.

Furthermore, there is a particular kind of attention that is important in mindfulness. This is *interoceptive attention*, or attentiveness to the physical sensations of the body. The practice uses bodily sensations, such as your perception of breathing, to anchor your attention in the present moment. After all, each breath happens right now, not in the past or the future. A brain region called the *insula*, located beneath the temporal lobe, is associated with interoceptive attention. Mindfulness affects the insula, making it easier to focus attention on the bodily sensations occurring right now and to avoid getting carried away by autopilot thinking about the past or the future.

Reprogramming Autopilot

Mindfulness helps you avoid automatic thinking by improving the function of your attention networks. However, studies suggest mindfulness also specifically impacts the medial cortex and the default mode network, where autopilot is generated. By practicing mindfulness, your autopilot mode is reprogrammed. Before mindfulness, the natural tendency is for the default mode network and the medial cortex to take charge and lead you down a path of mind wandering and thinking about yourself. As you develop mindfulness skills, it will become simpler and easier to experience the present moment by way of insula-based focus on the breath and other bodily sensations.

Improving Emotional Regulation

In bipolar disorder, emotional regulation processes are not working correctly. Mindfulness directly affects the emotional production regions (the amygdala and basal ganglia) and the emotional control areas, such as the medial cortex.

Thus, mindfulness directly improves your ability to regulate your emotional states.

Moving On

While there is much still to be learned, you now know a lot about the bipolar brain and how mindfulness can rewire it. Knowing that there is good science supporting mindfulness can be valuable as you take up your mindfulness practice.

The take-home message from this chapter is that mindfulness modifies the areas of the brain that are not working correctly in bipolar disorder. Furthermore, mindfulness changes your brain so that it is easier to keep your attention in the present moment, move out of autopilot, and control your emotions.

It's time to move on to developing a mindfulness practice. In the next chapter, you will learn more about meditation and your eight-step mindfulness recovery plan.

chapter 3

---

mindfulness and self-compassion

This chapter talks about the need for compassion, especially self-compassion, as you develop your mindfulness practice. Having self-compassion will help you reduce the symptoms of bipolar disorder as you use mindfulness to stay present with uncomfortable thoughts and emotions. The chapter opens with a discussion about the meaning of compassion and how it applies to mindfulness and bipolar disorder. It ends with some more details about the eight-step recovery plan that you will start using in chapter 4.

Compassion for Your Bipolar Self

Having compassion for yourself and for others is fundamental to the practice of mindfulness. But what does this mean? Compassion means being aware of someone's suffering and having a desire to help relieve that suffering. Applied to yourself, it means that you are fully aware of your own suffering and also have a desire to feel better. This book is about relieving the suffering associated with bipolar disorder. Specifically, it is about helping you relieve your own suffering.

Compassionate Awareness

One part of self-compassion is awareness of your own suffering. What does it mean to be completely aware of your own suffering? Mindfulness defines suffering broadly and includes feelings of dissatisfaction, unhappiness, and the sense that maybe things aren't quite right. So suffering can include the painful emotions and negative thinking patterns of bipolar disorder as well as feelings of discontentment, disappointment with life, and lack of joy that are often associated with this illness.

The first step toward self-compassion is being fully aware of your own suffering. You might be thinking something like, *But I'm already too focused on my unhappiness. I want to think more positively.* That seems logical. But in reality most of us have only a general sense of our own suffering. We don't consciously think much about the details; usually, we avoid thinking about them altogether. It's not much fun to think about the dissatisfactions in life. Instead, we often have a vague sense that we are unhappy, but we aren't sure why. Does that description fit for you?

The mindful approach is to be fully aware of and present with reality—just as it is—in each moment. That means being fully aware of your own suffering. You'll understand this better as you move through this chapter. Being present with your bipolar thoughts and emotions is an essential step on the path toward feeling better. After all, you can't change something that you don't understand. Most importantly, you have to avoid autopilot responses that increase your suffering. That requires being fully present with whatever exists in the moment. In particular, it means being able to be fully present with the symptoms of bipolar disorder, which will prevent autopilot from taking control and making things worse.

Compassionate Desire

The other part of self-compassion is the wish to relieve your own suffering. This desire is crucial. Sometimes autopilot thinking may tell you that you can't feel better or that you don't deserve to feel better. Again, it's important to recognize that these thoughts are just thoughts. Thoughts are not facts. Sometimes thoughts have truth in them, and sometimes they don't. No matter what your thoughts may be, you can feel better. All of us deserve to be happy and free from suffering.

Please take a moment right now and commit to relieving your own suffering from bipolar disorder. Commit to feeling better by practicing mindfulness.

Before moving on, here is one more thought about compassion. We humans are imperfect creatures. We make many mistakes. Bipolar disorder can cause behaviors that may lead to feelings of guilt or shame. However, none of us signed up for a psychiatric disorder. No one signed up for thinking patterns that cause problems. Part of becoming mindful is really seeing your imperfections for what they are, simply the nature of being human and living your life. Please be kind and gentle with yourself as you proceed.

• Liz's Story

Liz has been practicing mindfulness for about two years. She started right after she was diagnosed with bipolar disorder. As she started to become more mindfully aware of her thoughts and emotions, she noticed that critical thoughts came up in response to what she was thinking and feeling. She was thinking about her thinking, which is a classic example of autopilot. Liz would notice that she was thinking negative thoughts, and then she would think, *I shouldn't be thinking that way; that's really stupid.* Other times she observed that when she was feeling depressed, she would think, *I have no reason to be depressed right now. I shouldn't be feeling this way.*

Liz discovered that she was frequently getting stuck in an autopilot thinking cycle, in which distressing thoughts or emotions brought on more unpleasant thoughts, which led to even more uncomfortable thoughts and emotions (see figure 2.3). This is one of the main problems with autopilot thinking: it usually leads only to more autopilot thinking, not to solutions. To break out of that cycle, the first step is to completely accept reality as it is in the moment. For Liz, this meant accepting that she was thinking negatively or feeling depressed, rather than criticizing herself. It meant just being present with her thoughts and feelings. This at first seemed like the opposite of what she should do. After all, she wanted to find a way to spend less time feeling depressed and thinking negatively, right?

Right, but it turns out that the first step toward that goal was actually to accept the reality of the moment. We each have only two choices about reality, acceptance or resistance. Notice that changing reality is not an option, because we can't change the reality of the moment—it already exists. Think about this for a minute, because it is a key concept of mindfulness. If you notice that you are feeling depressed, you already have those feelings, right now, in the present moment. If you observe a negative thought, you have already had it. We may be able to change the future, but we can't change what's happening right now. By the time we become aware of it, the thought, emotion, sight, or sound has already happened. It is unchangeable. So, that leaves us with one of two choices: resistance or acceptance.

Resistance leads to suffering. Liz found that she was resisting thoughts or feelings that had already happened. She was doing this by criticizing her thoughts and feelings. This resistance was in the form of autopilot thoughts of *I shouldn't be thinking or feeling this way.* That resistance caused her to feel worse, because she was feeling bad about feeling bad. That's what autopilot does. This is the other main problem with autopilot thinking: it is usually unhelpful, and it often makes bipolar symptoms worse.

The mindful solution is acceptance. Liz found that by accepting reality, she could move on and not get stuck in a cycle of autopilot thinking. She found it was helpful to say to herself, *Oh, I'm having feelings of depression right now. I don't like it, but I can accept it and move on. I don't need to judge my feelings.*

Being Present with Bipolar Thoughts and Emotions

Mindfulness is about the compassionate acceptance of whatever exists in the present moment. This doesn't mean being passive; in fact, it's the opposite. From the clear view of mindful awareness, you can see the best course of action. Often, that action is doing something specific to feel better. Acceptance doesn't mean that you have to like or agree with whatever exists, either. It just means you accept it so that you can move on and not get stuck in autopilot thinking.

With acceptance comes the ability to be fully present with bipolar thoughts and emotions. As you will discover, letting negative thoughts and unpleasant feelings simply be there often results in their fading away. In fact, they are much more likely to fade away if you give them permission to be present. If you try to push them away, they will usually just spring back into awareness. See if this is true as you start to practice mindful awareness. In addition, mindful acceptance is the key to avoiding autopilot thinking. Autopilot thinking is often about wanting the present reality to be different from how it is. In other words, it's about resistance. Mindfulness short-circuits that thinking pattern.

Meditation as a Mindfulness Framework

Mindfulness is simply staying aware of the present moment, in other words, keeping your attention on the sights, sounds, sensations, thoughts, and emotions that are occurring right now. This is in contrast to autopilot, when your mind is deciding where your attention will be focused without your making a conscious decision about it.

Liz was on autopilot when she automatically started criticizing her own thoughts and emotions. She didn't make a conscious decision to do that; it just happened. Usually she didn't even notice that it was happening. She was carried away in the fast-flowing stream of her thoughts. As her mindfulness practice developed, however, she started to frequently notice when she was stuck in an autopilot thinking pattern. Today, she can use a short meditation (which you will learn in chapter 5) to move into mindful awareness. From a mindful perspective, she is able to decide if she needs to take any action to help herself feel better. Sometimes all she has to do is go on with her day.

Mindfulness is a very simple concept. We are all familiar with the idea of living in the moment—no rocket science required here. The problem is that our minds don't want to stay focused on the present. Our minds want to wander on autopilot. We have to train the mind to be able to stay mindfully aware. That is where meditation comes in.

Meditation is just keeping your attention where you want it. For example, a meditation could be focusing your awareness on the physical sensations of breathing. You can actually do this anywhere or anytime. You don't need to sit on a cushion on the floor with your legs crossed or go to a meditation center. However, you do need a formal daily meditation practice to train your attention. You can start practicing mindfulness meditation today in your own home. The meditation practices offered in this book can all be done sitting in a chair that is anywhere free from distractions, and the next chapter will give you step-by-step instructions.

Meditation also can be more complicated; some meditation traditions have various complex rituals and styles of meditation. But ultimately, all meditation practices have one thing in common: they are training your attention to stay where you want it. Mindfulness meditation is just keeping your attention focused on the present moment, being fully present with your life, breath by breath. But again, your mind will want to wander on autopilot, so keeping your attention focused is a skill that you have to learn. That's what meditation practice does. As discussed in chapter 2, practicing meditation rewires your brain through neuroplasticity. This makes it easier to keep your focus on the present, even when your brain wants to ruminate about the past or worry about the future.

Your Eight-Step Mindfulness Recovery Plan

Your mindfulness recovery plan for bipolar disorder is divided into eight steps, and chapters 4 through 11 each introduce one step in this plan. Each step builds upon the previous one, so it's important to work through these chapters sequentially.

Step 1. Your Daily Meditation Practice

Learning to practice sitting meditation on a daily basis is the first step in your bipolar recovery plan. In chapter 4, you will learn how to do a sitting meditation with focus on the breath. This will be the foundation for the rest of your practice. The sitting meditation is one of two types of meditations that you will learn in this book. The other type is a short, unscheduled meditation that you can use anytime you need to get out of autopilot. This is what you'll learn how to do in step 2.

Step 2. Targeting Bipolar Depression

As you have learned, autopilot thinking patterns can bring on bipolar depression or make it worse. Again, the way out of these autopilot thinking patterns is to move into a mental state of mindful awareness, which will permit you to get some distance from your autopilot thoughts so that they become much less powerful and less apt to cause depression. Rather than be swept away by the rapid stream of your thoughts, you will be able to watch them as they flow by. Chapter 5 introduces a short meditation, the mindful minute, to help you enter this mental state. You can take a minute to do this meditation whenever you are feeling depressed. You also can use the mindful minute when you are experiencing other unpleasant emotions, or any time you notice your mind on autopilot. The mindful minute and the sitting meditation with focus on the breath will form the groundwork of your mindfulness practice.

Step 3. Calming the Anxiety of Bipolar Disorder

Most people with bipolar disorder experience anxiety, and an autopilot thinking response to anxiety almost always makes it worse. The best way to manage anxiety is to cultivate the ability to be present with it rather than try to make it go away. While anxiety feels dreadful, it can't hurt you, and it will go away on its own if you can avoid the autopilot responses that will make it worse. Chapter 6 will teach you to sit in meditation with anxiety and let it fade away without your needing to do anything about it. This skill is a key component of your mindfulness practice. You will learn to use this approach with other symptoms of bipolar disorder as well.

Step 4: Observing Your Thinking Patterns

Chapter 7 tackles the autopilot thinking patterns that contribute to depression, anxiety, and irritability, and also addresses the negative thinking and low self-esteem of bipolar disorder. Step 4 will guide you in deepening your meditation practice as you become an observer of your own thoughts. You will practice keeping your attention in the present moment and watching your thoughts come and go. Watching your thoughts and discovering how your mind works is an important component of your meditation practice. In many meditation practices, the term *monkey mind* is used to describe how our minds chatter away. As you observe the monkey in your head, you will see how the chattering is often neither rational nor logical.

Step 5. Working with Mania and Desire

Desire is a very powerful emotion for everyone. We all struggle with wanting things that are either out of reach or maybe not good for us. For those with bipolar disorder, one of the most challenging symptoms is the intense desire that can occur with mania or hypomania. In chapter 8, you will practice being present with desire. You will learn that you can watch desire and cravings as they come and go and that there's no need to act on these feelings. This practice also helps us discover that obtaining what we desire won't necessarily make us happy. We discover that desires are thoughts and emotions that often simply arise and pass and have very little meaning.

Step 6. Managing Irritability and Anger

Irritability and anger are common symptoms of bipolar disorder and can occur during both depression and mania. Chapter 9 focuses on the feeling of aversion, which is what we experience when we don't like something. Aversion often underlies emotions of frustration and rage. In chapter 9, you will use mindfulness to work with these difficult emotions and develop a new relationship with them.

Step 7. Rethinking Your Bipolar Self

Autopilot thinking patterns tend to be self-critical during depression. In contrast, your self-esteem can be too high during mania. In chapter 10, you will develop a new relationship with your thoughts about yourself. Thoughts about the self are just thoughts and often don't represent reality. Through mindful awareness, you will discover that you are perfect as you already are. You also will discover how mindfulness can enhance your compassion for yourself.

Step 8. Being Bipolar and Happy

Chapter 11 will help you discover the delight of being fully present with your life, breath by breath. Our autopilot thinking misleads us into believing that happiness is based upon external circumstances. In particular, we tend to believe that by obtaining certain things we will be happier; or we think that happiness is something absolute that will occur at some time in the future. Mindfulness teaches us that the mind is actually never satisfied. By practicing meditation and watching our thoughts and emotions, such as desire, we see that nothing we can ever get will make us happy for very long. We discover that desire is often just the endless chattering of the monkey mind. By developing the skill to relax in the present moment, we find that true joy and happiness already exist; we just need to create a space for them to manifest.

Getting Started

You now have all the background information you need to start your mindfulness practice. You may find it helpful on occasion to reread the material in part 1, especially as your mindfulness practice deepens. It's time to begin.

your mindfulness plan for solving the bipolar puzzle

chapter 4

---

your daily
meditation practice

T o solve the bipolar puzzle, the first thing you need is a daily mindfulness meditation practice. This chapter teaches you how to do a sitting meditation that will serve as the foundation for your mindfulness practice. As you sit, you will focus on the breath. Subsequent chapters will focus on the main symptoms of bipolar disorder and give you some additional meditations to address these symptoms. The sitting meditation described here will serve as a basis for everything that comes later. This chapter begins with a discussion about why regular practice in your bipolar recovery plan is so important.

Practicing Regularly

Meditation is a skill you have to learn. It's just like learning to read or ride a bike or play a video game. As with all skills, the more you practice, the more skillful you become. Regular practice rewires the brain through neuroplasticity (see chapter 2). That rewiring makes it easier for you to keep your attention focused on the present moment. It also helps you notice when you are on autopilot, so you can effortlessly move into mindful awareness. This will help you avoid the autopilot thinking scripts that worsen bipolar symptoms and contribute to stress, dissatisfaction, and unhappiness.

You know from your own experience that your mind wants to stay on autopilot, either ruminating about the past or planning for the future. These ruminations worsen bipolar symptoms. Again, mindfulness meditation is simply focusing your attention on the sights, sounds, and sensations of the present moment.

The meditation practice offered in this chapter really boils down to noticing when you are on autopilot and then shifting your attention back to the present moment. You repeat this process over and over again. Autopilot will always be with you, but you can get better and better at noticing it and shining the spotlight of your attention on the present moment. To use an analogy, if you were to go to the gym and lift weights, you would call each time you raise the dumbbell a repetition or a rep. As you do the reps, you are strengthening your muscles. In mindfulness meditation, you are doing reps as you notice that you are on autopilot and gently guide your attention back to the here and now. You need to practice regularly to improve so that you will be able to refocus your attention on the here and now when you really need to—that is, when you experience a bipolar symptom, such as depression, anxiety, or irritability. In other words, you need to strengthen your meditation muscle, so it can perform the work of solving the bipolar puzzle.

Watching Your Expectations

One benefit of practicing mindfulness meditation and seeing how the mind works is that you'll notice how thoughts often take the form of expectations and judgments. Practicing also helps us see that these expectations and judgments often lead to unhappiness and dissatisfaction when our expectations are not met or when we judge something as being unsatisfactory.

As you start to practice, I invite you to notice if you have expectations about what meditation may be like. In particular, notice if you expect to achieve a calm, quiet mind. It won't happen very often. There may be times when your mind is quiet, but for most of us, that isn't very common.

Also, notice the tendency of the mind to judge. See if you tend to judge your meditation experiences as either good or bad, because you have expectations about what you think meditation should be like. If you tend to do this, I encourage you just to be fully present with each meditation session. You do not need to label it in any particular way.

Your meditation practice is a laboratory where you can conduct experiments about your life. As with a scientific experiment, the goal is to approach your practice with curiosity and openness. If you notice that expectations and judgments occur around your meditation practice, you may then be able to see how they show up in other areas of your life. As you watch your mind, you will discover that expectations and judgments are mostly just the chattering of your monkey mind and serve only to make you unhappy and dissatisfied.

Choosing a Daily Practice

Sitting meditation with focus on the breath is just that: sitting and keeping attention on the physical sensations of the breath. Most meditation practitioners refer to this as *sitting*, which is the term used throughout this book.

There are many other meditations that you could potentially use for your daily practice. One isn't better than another, but you may find that you like some more than others. As you gain experience, you can experiment. The most important thing is to find meditations that you like and look forward to practicing.

That said, the meditation you are going to learn now should be your starting point. You will use several variations of it throughout the rest of the book. Later on, you also may want to experiment with some options provided in the appendix. (And online—download guided audio versions of the practices offered in this book at http://www.newharbin ger.com/31854.)

This chapter will help you work out the details of your meditation practice: when and where you will practice, how long you will meditate for, and how you will sit and breathe. But first, Ann's story may give you some insight into how to go about getting started.

• Ann's Story

Ann is thirty-two and has bipolar II disorder. She was first diagnosed when she was twenty-one. She has taken a number of medications over the years. About five years ago, she and her prescriber found a combination that works well. Ann has been mostly free of mood symptoms since then, but she still experiences intermittent depression. When depressed, Ann is also very anxious. Anxiety keeps her awake at night, and she worries excessively. Sometimes she has out-of-the-blue attacks of anxiety with rapid heartbeat, and feels like she can't breathe.

Ann started a mindfulness meditation practice to help with her autopilot thinking patterns that increase her anxiety. She has found that it also helps with her depression and stress.

When she started to meditate, one of Ann's biggest challenges was sitting on a regular basis. This isn't unusual. Most people struggle with that to some degree. Ann found that having a regular time set aside each day to sit helped her keep up a daily practice. The key for her was finding a time of day that fit with her schedule. She tried meditating first thing in the morning, but on weekdays she felt pressured to get ready to go to work and found it was really difficult to settle into meditation. Weekend mornings were also problematic, because she found herself wanting to get going with her day rather than wanting to take time out to meditate. She then experimented with sitting right before bed each night. That didn't work well either, because she had trouble staying awake. After some experimentation, Ann found that the best time to sit during the week was right after getting home from work. The best time on weekends was early afternoon. Once she committed to those times, she had no trouble keeping up a regular practice.

Ann lives alone, and her only companion is a cat. For her, finding a spot to sit was no problem. Her favorite room was her bedroom. She started practicing there and found that the space worked really well. Ann ended up using a specific corner in her bedroom to sit. She added an incense burner and a candle to support her practice.

Finding the right amount of time to practice was challenging, as it can be for many people. When she first started practicing, Ann noticed that after about five minutes she wanted the meditation to be over. What worked for her in the beginning was to commit to five minutes. As she became more familiar with sitting, she was able to gradually increase the amount of practice time, and now that she has been meditating for over a year, she finds that she can easily sit for thirty minutes at a time.

Planning Your Practice

As you work out your meditation schedule, you need to choose a certain time of day to practice regularly. Most people prefer to sit first thing in the morning or last thing at night, but your favorite time could be the late afternoon or some other time. Like Ann, you can experiment initially until you find the time that works best for you. You may want to start with either early morning or late evening and see how it works. You can experiment with other times, if necessary, to discover what works best, but please try to find a specific time to sit daily. Almost all of us are more consistent in our practice if we commit to practice meditation at a certain time each day.

Where to Meditate

Your sitting environment needs to be free from distractions, such as your mobile phone, computer, or TV, and interruptions by others. You may find that having several different places to practice works well for you, or maybe you will prefer to stick with one spot. You can sit indoors or outside. Ideas include a corner of your bedroom, like Ann uses, or a park bench.

If you do not live alone, finding a quiet place to sit in the home can be challenging. This may be particularly true if you have young children. This may be another reason to practice late at night, after the kids are in bed. It's important to talk with other family members, so they support your practice and do not disturb you while you're sitting.

If you live with other people, you will probably want to choose a room that others can easily stay out of for a while. The kitchen is not a good choice, obviously. Please take some time to think through what might work best in your situation.

You don't really have to do anything special to practice mindfulness meditation. All you need is a comfortable place to sit in an area that is conducive to practice. But if you find some items to enhance your sitting, like pictures of peaceful scenery or a small gong to strike to start your practice, then, by all means, use those.

You may be wondering, *How quiet does my sitting space need to be?* It doesn't have to be absolutely quiet. For example, many people enjoy meditating outdoors, and if you are up in the mountains or out in the desert, there are all kinds of nature noises, such as wind blowing or birds singing. Many people find these sounds to be soothing and supportive of their practice while human noise can be more disturbing. But most of us have difficulty finding a space that is completely noise-free. Ultimately, your practice will be about experiencing whatever is there in each moment. With time, you can learn to be mindful no matter what is going on. As you start your practice, you can work with some noise by just being aware of it and not getting carried away with thinking about it.

Finally, in addition to sitting by yourself, you can experiment with sitting with others. Most communities have meditation centers where you can practice with like-minded individuals. Most of us find that sitting with a group is much easier than sitting alone.

How Long to Practice

Be gentle with yourself as you start your practice. My meditation teacher says, "Stop sitting when you feel like you could sit for five more minutes." In other words, don't push yourself so hard that you won't want to sit again tomorrow.

That said, it is important to have a specific duration for each sitting session. I strongly recommend using some type of timer. You can use a kitchen timer or a clock with an alarm or your smartphone app. Set the timer and then put the device somewhere out of sight, so you won't be tempted to keep peeking at it.

Try starting in the five- to ten-minute range for your first few times and then adjust upward based upon how it goes. Five minutes is probably the minimum amount of time for a meditation session to be helpful. I would strongly encourage working your way up to ten to fifteen minutes per session within a few weeks. Eventually you may find that some sessions can be for twenty to thirty minutes. The maximum for most of us should be thirty-five to forty minutes.

Sitting Posture

Thinking about meditation may conjure up images of people sitting on a cushion on the floor in the lotus position. The full lotus position is where the legs are crossed and the feet are on top of opposite thighs. It looks very uncomfortable. Trust me, it is. My own practice is in the Soto Zen tradition. We do sit on cushions on the floor in a specific posture, but most of us don't sit in full lotus. Many of us sit in a pose known as Burmese position, which is much more comfortable than the lotus position. In Burmese pose, you sit on a cushion, called a *zafu*, which is on top of a thick mat called a *zabuton*. Our bottoms are on the zafu, and we cross one leg in front of the other on the zabuton (see figure 4.1). The Burmese pose is an excellent sitting position, and you may want to learn to use it as your practice develops (see the appendix for full instructions for the Burmese pose). Ann started sitting in a chair but now usually meditates in the Burmese position. Whatever position you choose, the important thing is to find what works for you.

Figure 4.1: Burmese Meditation Pose

The wonderful thing about mindfulness is that you can be aware of the present moment in absolutely any posture. That said, sitting quietly and comfortably will help you develop and deepen your meditation practice. You will start off sitting in a chair (see figure 4.2). All the meditations in this book (except the walking meditation in the appendix) can be done sitting in a chair. However, if you decide to learn the Burmese pose, feel free to sit that way for any of the meditations in this book.

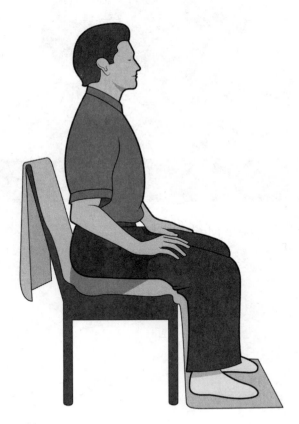

Figure 4.2: Sitting Meditation in a Chair

As you can see from figure 4.2, it's important to sit in a very upright posture. Your chair needs to be firm, like a dining room chair. Your comfy, overstuffed TV chair will not work well. You may find it helpful to have a cushion on the floor for your feet. Some people find sitting with a cushion on the chair works well too. If you try this, the cushion should be firm, and your feet still need to reach the floor. Sit with your back straight and not touching the chair back. Both feet should be flat on the floor, and your hands should rest comfortably in your lap. Your head should be up and facing straight ahead with your chin slightly tucked.

Keeping your back straight is critically important. Start by raising your back so that it is straight and the rest of your body hangs on your skeleton. As you settle in before you start your meditation, take a few moments to relax your muscles.

Your eyes can be open or closed. If they're open, they should be about half-closed and focused loosely on the floor a few feet in front of you. Experiment and find out what works best for you.

Finally, respect and honor your body. If the pose described above is impractical for you because of your body type or because of certain medical conditions, then feel free to modify it so that it works for you.

Focusing on the Breath

The breath serves as an anchor for your meditation. When you focus on the physical sensations of the breath, your attention is automatically fixated on the present moment. Your breathing occurs right now, not in the past or the future. The breath is also always with you, so it is constantly available as an anchor any time that you want to practice mindfulness meditation. It's very handy that way.

Besides the breath, there are other anchors you can use. One example is focusing awareness on all the physical sensations of the body (see chapter 5). This is the anchor used in the more advanced meditation known as open mindful awareness, during which you pay attention to the physical sensations of the breath and the body as well as to the sights, sounds, thoughts, and emotions of each moment. An open awareness meditation is included in the appendix.

As mentioned, one way mindfulness helps you cope better with the symptoms of bipolar disorder is that it allows you to gain some distance on your thoughts and emotions; as a result, they lose power and become less distressing. You gain this distance on your thoughts and emotions as you move out of autopilot and into the present moment. It can be difficult to break out of autopilot, especially if you are upset or experiencing the strong emotions of bipolar disorder. At those times, you need a very secure anchor for your meditation. Your breath is that anchor. You keep coming back to focus on your breathing so you can stay in the present moment.

Sitting Meditation with Focus on the Breath

The sitting meditation with focus on the breath is your foundation for solving the bipolar puzzle. Follow these instructions step-by-step. You may want to read the instructions first and then put them into practice. A guided audio version of this meditation is also available online at http://www.newharbinger.com/31854.

Preparation: *Make sure you have everything you need in your meditation space. You will need a firm chair and a timer. Do whatever you need to do to avoid distractions. For example, close the door and turn off your phone, the TV, and any music. Tell family members that you will be sitting, so they will know not to disturb you. Set your timer for five minutes. (You can increase the time as you become more familiar with this practice.)*

Posture: *Sit upright with your back straight (figure 4.2). Your feet should be flat on the floor and your hands relaxed in your lap. Take a moment to really straighten your back. Then relax the muscles throughout your body. Close your eyes or loosely focus on the floor a few feet in front of you.*

Focusing attention on the breath: *Shine the spotlight of your attention on the physical sensations of breathing. These include the rising and falling of the chest, the expanding and contracting of the abdomen, and the air coming into the nose and then going back out. There are many other subtle sensations that you will notice as you start paying attention to your breathing. It is okay to shift your attention from one breathing sensation to another or to keep your awareness on whatever is most noticeable. Your aim is simply to be aware of and keep your attention on the breath. The goal is not to change the breath in any way; the breath is just your* anchor to keep you in the present moment. If you discover that your breath changes as you observe it, that's okay. Just observe what happens. You don't need to fix or change anything.

Counting your breath: A helpful technique is to count each breath cycle. Count one for the first inhalation and exhalation cycle, two for the next, and so on. Count to ten and then start over. If you lose count, and you will, then start over. You can practice this meditation both counting and not counting. Spending time counting may be more helpful in your first few weeks of practice than later on. As your practice develops, try to spend more time not counting and just being aware of the breath.

Mind wandering: Your mind will go on autopilot and wander. That is what minds do. It's in their job description. Though you will have some meditation sessions in which your mind is mostly calm and autopilot seems to be turned off, most of the time you will be sitting with autopilot. Again, the goal is not to eliminate autopilot, but to recognize when it is happening and be able to move into mindful awareness. It may seem counterintuitive, but the more the mind wanders, the more you get to practice noticing it and shifting into mindfulness, which is good. Whenever you notice you are on autopilot, thinking about the past or future, just quietly escort your attention back to the breath and the present moment. If you are upset or feeling strong emotion, the pull of autopilot will be stronger. This is also good. In response to your mind's resistance to staying in the present moment, your mindfulness muscle will grow stronger. Just keep coming back to the breath.

Drowsiness: You might start to feel sleepy. This is not uncommon. You should work with drowsiness the same way that you work with autopilot thinking. Notice what's happening without frustration, and tenderly guide your awareness back to the breath.

Ending your meditation: *When the timer goes off, transition your attention back to your sitting space. Take your time and maybe stretch a little. Congratulate yourself! Think about your experience.*

That was the sitting meditation with focus on the breath. I hope you enjoyed it. You may not always enjoy your sitting sessions. Please know that there are no bad or good meditations. Mindfulness meditation is about being aware of reality, moment by moment. Whatever happens during your meditation is part of the practice. You will learn something about how your mind works from whatever you experience when you sit.

Now that you know the basics, please proceed to use this meditation at least once a day. You will miss some days, and that's okay. But if you can sit most days, even for a short meditation, the consistency will really strengthen your practice.

Moving Forward

Meditation is about seeing how your mind works. You won't always like what you observe. However, none of us signed up for the thinking patterns that we developed over the years. Autopilot is a product of genetic predisposition and life experiences. Ann has found it helpful to think about her autopilot scripts in the third person. She will say to herself, "There goes Ann on an autopilot rant about her mother again." That helps her attain some distance from her thinking patterns and not get carried away with them. It also helps her to acknowledge some of her well-worn thinking ruts with a smile. You may want to try this too.

Do not be surprised if you experience some psychological resistance to practicing. The mind resists meditation, especially in the beginning. When you notice that you don't want to sit, you can acknowledge this without judgment. It can be helpful to give voice to the resistance. You may want to try saying aloud, "I don't want to sit today, because..." Recognize that there may be logic behind your reasoning, but also recognize that most often what you are experiencing is psychological resistance. Notice how powerful this resistance can be. Then go ahead and sit anyway.

Again, be gentle and compassionate with yourself in your sitting. Meditation is not about being hard on yourself. Meditation practice is imperfect, like life itself. None of us sit as much or as long as we think we should. I invite you to sit with an attitude of compassion, nonjudgmental curiosity, and a sense of humor.

chapter 5

targeting bipolar depression

Now that you have started your daily meditation practice, you can begin to focus specifically on the symptoms of bipolar disorder. This chapter focuses on bipolar depression and introduces the mindful minute meditation as a method for moving out of the kind of autopilot thinking that can cause bipolar depression or make it worse. What you learn in this chapter can be applied to other bipolar symptoms as well. This chapter begins with John's story to illustrate how mindfulness can help you recognize your autopilot thinking.

• *John's Story*

John has had bipolar I disorder since he was a teenager. Like many people with this illness, he found that medication treatment was very effective for preventing manic episodes. However, for many years, he experienced chronic depression that just wouldn't go away. He was treated with several different medication combinations and psychotherapy, but he was still depressed at least half of the time.

Two years ago, John started a mindfulness practice. By becoming more aware of his thinking patterns, John discovered how autopilot thinking was keeping him depressed.

John was originally surprised to hear that we are typically unaware of our autopilot thinking patterns. When his mindfulness teacher first told him about autopilot, he didn't really believe it. John thought he was aware of what was going on in his head. He said,

"I'm the one thinking my thoughts, so of course I know what I'm thinking."

As he began practicing mindfulness, however, John started to notice very specific thinking patterns that were associated with his depression. He discovered that a thinking cycle would start when he experienced physical sensations of depression. For John, depression felt like a heavy sensation in his chest and stomach. It was almost like being nauseous. "It's really an awful feeling," he said.

John discovered that his automatic thinking response to his feelings of depression was to try to think of ways to get rid of them. He learned that the mind has a natural tendency to try to avoid emotional discomfort; this is the autopilot response.

You might think that John's thoughts would be helpful. After all, his autopilot response was trying to stop the feelings of depression. In fact, his thinking patterns might have been helpful if they actually had led to his doing something to help himself feel better. Sometimes autopilot thinking patterns can be helpful.

But after about a month of practicing mindfulness, John realized that his autopilot thinking patterns weren't helpful for his depression at all. He discovered that his mind would just go in circles, going over what he had tried in the past to help his depression and wondering if it had worked or not. This would lead to thinking about past episodes of depression and how long they had lasted. Then he might start worrying about how long the depression would last this time.

And so on. John realized that he got stuck in these same autopilot thinking ruts, time after time. He also discovered that his thinking never led to his taking any action. Rather, it only led to more thinking. Most importantly, he discovered that the more that he thought about his depression, the worse he felt. This realization was a major breakthrough for John.

John's story is very typical. Almost everyone with bipolar depression has autopilot thinking patterns that make their depression worse. The first step in addressing these patterns is to recognize them. One of the main purposes of your daily meditation practice is to help you start to recognize your autopilot patterns. When you sit focusing attention on the breath, you will notice your mind wandering off on autopilot. Each time you notice and bring your attention back to the present moment, you become better at recognizing when this happens. As your practice skills develop, you will be able to recognize autopilot in your daily life as well, when you are not actually practicing meditation.

Recognizing the Role of Autopilot

Mindfulness is about developing the ability to maintain awareness of the present moment. With your attention focused on the present, you will be aware of the sights, sounds, and sensations that are happening right now. In contrast, when you are in your normal autopilot state, your mind is on the past or future, and you are unaware of many of the sensations of each moment.

Try this simple experiment. Take a few deep breaths and then focus on the physical sensations of your body. Do a short scan by focusing attention briefly on your lower body and then your upper body. Start with your feet and work upward gradually through your legs, your torso, your arms, your neck and head. What did you discover? Most likely you noticed physical sensations that you aren't normally aware of, such as clothing against your skin or the pressure of the chair in which you're sitting against your back. Mindfulness brings about awareness of sensations that you might not notice in your normal unmindful state. Similarly, it can bring about greater awareness of your autopilot thinking patterns.

Like John, you may believe that you usually are aware of your own thoughts. It seems like we know what we are thinking. In one sense we do. We have an experience of our thoughts as they happen. But when we're on autopilot, we are carried away by our thoughts. We think about one thing and then another and then another. Our attention is focused on whatever the thought is at the moment. What we don't see is the big picture. As a result, we miss the autopilot thinking patterns.

In mindful awareness, we can see thoughts as they come and go. We start to see the autopilot patterns. We start to recognize the thinking ruts that we get stuck in time after time.

As you can see from John's story, our autopilot thinking is our mind's way of trying to relieve our pain, but the problem is that we often get stuck in thinking patterns that don't result in any helpful actions, and frequently, these thinking patterns actually make our symptoms worse (see figure 2.3). As you start to notice the autopilot thinking patterns that make your depression worse, you also can use a practice that I call "the mindful minute," which I'll describe later in this chapter, to make yourself feel better. The mindful minute is a short meditation that I developed to help you move out of autopilot and into mindful awareness. It was inspired by the three-minute breathing space taught in MBCT (Segal, Williams, and Teasdale 2002).

How to Move Out of Autopilot

John found that practicing the mindful minute when depressed made a big difference in his life. His feelings of depression continued to come up, but by recognizing and breaking out of his autopilot thinking patterns, John found that those feelings usually faded away quickly. He further discovered that from the perspective of mindful awareness, he could take positive action to feel better. For example, he found that taking a short walk or listening to music would almost always lead to a happier mood.

The first step in moving out of autopilot is to recognize it. Starting right now, you can begin to work on noticing when you are on autopilot. Pay special attention to the autopilot patterns that come up when you are feeling depressed. When you begin to notice these patterns, you also can use the mindful minute (described later in this chapter) to move out of autopilot and into mindfulness.

Accepting the Reality of the Moment

Though the aim of mindfulness is to feel better, the first step is always acceptance of the reality of the moment. This is the single most important concept of mindfulness. Autopilot wants things to be different. In regard to bipolar depression, the aim of autopilot thinking is to escape from emotional discomfort. But again, as John discovered, the problem is that autopilot thinking almost always makes things worse.

The only way out of the autopilot trap is complete and total acceptance of your current emotional state, no matter how painful it is. Another way to think about this is that you stay fully present with the reality of the moment. This is hard, but it's absolutely necessary. How do you do that? You acknowledge your current feelings and then relax with them. Your only aim at this point is to be completely present with and fully experience the reality of the moment. Your mind will resist this and try to keep going back on autopilot. Your job is to keep moving back into mindful awareness using the mindful minute. John found that sometimes he would have to do this over and over again until the autopilot thinking cycle was broken. It's okay to use the mindful minute as often as you need to.

Getting a Better View

In addition to making bipolar depression worse, autopilot thinking obscures our view of reality. For example, John discovered that his autopilot thinking about depression included a belief that his depression wouldn't go away and that nothing he could do would make him feel any better. He wasn't consciously aware of that belief, however, until he started paying close attention to his autopilot thinking. This belief clouded his view of reality. From a perspective of mindful awareness, he could see that his depressive symptoms tended to come and go, but from his autopilot perspective, it seemed that he would be stuck in depression forever.

Please start paying attention to your own autopilot thinking to see if you have any beliefs that may be muddying your view of reality about your depression.

Mindfulness helps us see that our viewpoint provides only partial truth, at best. This is important, because we tend to believe that our own perspective is unquestionably true. A simple example is being in a room with several people standing in a circle. Each person has a different view of the room and of the other people in the room. The person across from you can see what's behind you, but you can't. Whose perception is right? Of course, you can see from this example that there is no right viewpoint. It's obvious that all perspectives can be considered correct, but each provides only partial truth.

What we often don't realize or remember, however, is that this principle holds true for all our perspectives, including the ones we have about ourselves. We never see the complete picture. Our views are biased by our own ideas and beliefs that color how we see the world.

Mindfulness gives you the choice to take action by letting go of the thinking ruts that keep you stuck. In John's case, mindful awareness liberated him from his entrenched beliefs about depression. He could see that his depression wasn't permanent and that he could do things to feel better. Watching his symptoms from a perspective of mindful awareness, John discovered that his level of depression wasn't consistent. In fact, he found that his depressive symptoms frequently faded away after a few minutes without him having to do anything.

Please use mindful awareness to find out if the same holds true for you.

Watching Your Symptoms Fade Away

Most people with bipolar depression discover that their symptoms wax and wane throughout the day. After practicing mindfulness for a while, many people also discover that feelings of depression are more likely to fade away if they are allowed just to be. Emotions are like disobedient children; they tend to do the opposite of what you want. If you try to push symptoms of depression away, they will almost always push back. But if you let them be, they will usually diminish. See if this is true for you.

The next section will give you a new mindfulness tool to help you with bipolar depression and other symptoms. Before moving on, though, here's a quick review of three ways in which mindfulness can help with depression. First, mindfulness is how you can break out of the autopilot thinking that worsens depression. Second, mindfulness gives you a clear view of reality, so you can take actions that are appropriate for the situation and that will help you feel better. Third, mindful acceptance of depressive symptoms makes them more likely to fade away without your needing to do anything at all. With this is mind, it's time to learn how to do the mindful minute.

Using the Mindful Minute

You can use this meditation almost anywhere and in most situations. You don't need to do anything special to get ready. Just use it whenever you notice feelings of depression. It can be done sitting or standing and with eyes open or closed. Finally, you don't need to time this meditation. It's called the mindful minute, but you can take as much time as you need. Most people find that five minutes is about right. Use the mindful minute as often as you need to. If depressive symptoms persist, you may want to keep repeating it.

The Mindful Minute Meditation

The purpose of this short meditation is to move out of autopilot and into mindful awareness in response to depressive symptoms. The meditation has three steps. Read through the steps and then do the meditation. A guided audio version of this meditation is also available online. (Visit at http://www.newharbinger .com/31854 to access the file; you can find more details at the very end of this book.)

Step 1. *Begin to move into mindfulness by doing a short meditation with your attention focused on the breath. This is just a very short version of the daily meditation that you learned in chapter 4. As you do this short meditation, count your breath cycles or* just keep your attention on the physical sensations of your breath. Your mind will likely want to keep going back on autopilot. That's okay. It's what our minds do. But pay close attention and gently direct your attention back to the physical sensations of the breath whenever your mind wanders.

Step 2. Once you feel anchored in the present moment, take an inventory of your current situation. Your aim is to find out what is going on with your body, what autopilot scripts are running in your head, and the current state of your mood. You can use the acronym BAM to remember this: body, autopilot, and mood. First, do a quick scan of your body to discover if you are experiencing physical sensations of depression, such as a sick feeling in the pit of your stomach. Also notice if you have tight muscles, pain, or other discomfort. Next, check to see what autopilot scripts are running in your head. It may be helpful to label your thoughts—for example, I'm worrying about how long I will be depressed. You may want to say this out loud. Finally, notice what your current mood state is, such as depressed, irritable, worried, or happy. Again, it may be helpful to label your mood state: I'm feeling depressed right now.

Step 3. The final step is acknowledgment, acceptance, and presence. Make a conscious decision to completely accept the reality of the moment without trying to fix or change anything. You are making a commitment to be fully present with reality as it exists in this moment. Try to let everything be and to stay present with it, moment by moment. If you find you need an anchor to achieve this, you can focus some attention on your breath. Keep coming back to the breath as often as you need to. Try saying whatever is going on (either to yourself or out loud). If you are depressed, it could go something like this: "I feel depression in the pit of my stomach, and my muscles are tight. My autopilot scripts are *running about how long I will be depressed and about how much I don't like it. My mood is depressed, with some irritability. I fully acknowledge and completely accept my reality in this moment. I commit to be fully present with this reality." Try to consciously relax your muscles. Stay present with reality, breath by breath. You can end the meditation whenever you feel ready. Simply transition your attention back to your surroundings.*

After you do this meditation, you may see that there are some actions that you can take to feel better, or you may realize that you don't have to do anything. Sometimes merely breaking out of autopilot is all you need to do to feel better. Just being present with depression frequently leads to immediate symptom improvement. But if there are actions that you can take to help yourself, by all means take them.

Congratulations. You now have a second mindfulness tool to help you solve the bipolar puzzle. The mindful minute is an important tool to help you manage your depressive symptoms. It can be used with any bipolar symptom and at any time you notice that you are on autopilot. Please use it often. The more you practice mindfulness, the greater the benefit that you will receive.

Your Mindfulness Tools

You now have two mindfulness tools in your toolbox to help you solve the puzzle of living well with bipolar disorder. The first is your daily sitting meditation from chapter 4. The second tool is the mindful minute. I would recommend adding the mindful minute to your daily practice and doing it on a scheduled basis three times a day until you get used to it. Once you feel comfortable with the mindful minute, you can start using it whenever you notice feelings of depression.

A Few More Implements

Now would be a good time to make a list of what steps you might take to feel better after using the mindful minute. Trying to come up with action steps when you are feeling bad is like trying to develop a hotel evacuation plan when the hotel is on fire—not the best idea. Having this list handy can be helpful when you are feeling depressed, upset, or stressed.

So, I invite you to take a few minutes to think about what helps you feel better when you are experiencing symptoms of bipolar disorder. Keep this list with you, and pull it out if you need it after completing the mindful minute.

What You Will Learn Next

The next chapter will focus on the bipolar symptom of anxiety and talk more about staying present with uncomfortable emotional states.

Much of this book stresses the need to be present with reality regardless of whether you like it or not. I know this is scary and may not feel right. Trust me on this. The only way to solve the bipolar puzzle is to make friends with your symptoms. It is a radically different approach. But this is the solution to the bipolar puzzle.

calming bipolar anxiety

The mindful approach to symptoms of bipolar disorder is radically different from what the mind wants to do. Therefore, it may seem illogical and counterintuitive to you. The important thing to remember is that mindfulness works. You've already seen the evidence for the effectiveness of mindfulness (chapter 1) and how mindfulness can rewire the brain (chapter 2).

Again, our minds naturally don't want to feel emotional or physical pain. The brain is hardwired to protect you from pain. Resisting emotional pain is a reflex, like yanking your hand away from a hot stovetop. In some situations, this mechanism keeps you safe, but not when what you are resisting is being present with your bipolar symptoms. The problem is that trying to protect yourself often backfires, as John's story illustrated in chapter 5. One of the most important skills you will learn in this book is how to be present with unpleasant emotional states.

This chapter will focus on staying present with the unpleasant emotional state of anxiety. It may sound scary, but I promise you that once you experience this for yourself, you will see that there is no reason to be fearful. In fact, learning how to stay present with your bipolar symptoms is the key to liberation from your suffering. Even beyond the symptoms of bipolar disorder, the pathway to liberation from all suffering is to be present with reality, as it exists, moment by moment.

• Amy's Story

Like most people with bipolar disorder, Amy suffers with symptoms of anxiety. She started having episodes of depression when she was eighteen, and a few years later had her first manic episode. For the next few years, she had long periods of good symptom control. When she was twenty-five, she started to develop symptoms of anxiety. Her medications continued to prevent episodes of depression and mood elevations, but they were not very helpful for anxiety.

Amy experiences generalized anxiety. That is, she tends to worry a lot. Some days are almost completely consumed with excessive worry. She knows that her worries often aren't rational, but she can't stop. The worry and rumination keep her awake at night and interfere with her ability to concentrate. She often also finds herself feeling very irritable and distracted.

Amy started to practice mindfulness a few months ago, and over time, she has noticed that her anxiety doesn't bother her nearly as much as it did before she started meditating. With meditation, Amy began to pay close attention to her thoughts and was able to see that her worry was usually about trying to prevent emotional pain.

Though Amy always knew that she worried a lot, until she started practicing mindfulness, she really couldn't see the big picture of her worry and anxiety. She often was too caught up in her worries to be a good observer. With mindfulness, Amy became an observer of her own mind and realized that her worry was mostly about her mother. Amy's mother is in poor health and lives alone in another state. Amy talks to her by phone several times every week, but her mother is usually very vague about how she is doing.

The first thing Amy realized from her mindfulness practice was that most of her worry was about how her mother was really getting along. She noticed that she imagined all kinds of scenarios about her mother getting sick and not having anyone to help her. After coming up with these scenarios, she would spend hours thinking about what she could do to prevent them from happening. The problem was that her thinking went around and around in the same circles and never led to any solutions.

As her meditation practice deepened, Amy came to understand her anxiety at a deeper level. She realized that she was very afraid of losing her mother. She also recognized that she was terrified of the emotional pain she would experience with her mom's passing. She comprehended that her worry about her mother's situation was excessive and, most importantly, she recognized that her worry was really an attempt to avoid the pain that would come with her mother's eventual death. The worry was actually resistance to future emotional pain. This realization was a major breakthrough for Amy.

Recognizing Your Automatic Response

Our brains all respond the same way to uncomfortable thoughts and emotions. The autopilot response is to try to make the pain go away. That seems like it would be a good thing, and sometimes it works, but autopilot thinking responses often make our emotional discomfort worse. This is what Amy discovered, and it's probably true for you too.

One reason mindfulness works is that it allows us to see what is going on in our minds. By observing our thoughts and emotions, we discover which thinking patterns are helpful and which ones aren't. You may think that you already know what's going on in your mind, but as you start practicing mindfulness, you will find that you really weren't very aware at all.

Staying Present

Amy's story illustrates why you need to develop the ability to be present with unpleasant thoughts and emotions, such as anxiety. As you practice mindfulness, you will come to understand your own autopilot thinking patterns and how they may be trying to protect you from certain unpleasant thoughts and emotions.

Please pay particular attention to whether your thinking patterns are helpful for you. Autopilot thinking patterns can be useful. The problem is that they often are habitual ruts that we get stuck in, as Amy discovered.

Confronting Impermanence

Amy was struggling with one of the essential truths of life. Everything is impermanent. We exist for only a short time in this life. All of the things that we care about will pass on. Our autopilot tries to protect us from this reality. But, at some level, we all know the truth. Through our practice of mindfulness, we can come to terms with this, rather than try to pretend it doesn't exist. Being present with impermanence is the toll-free expressway to freedom from suffering. This path leads to the solution to the bipolar puzzle and the solution to the puzzle of all of our lives.

Relaxing with Not Knowing

Just as our fear of impermanence makes us uncomfortable, so does uncertainty. When we don't know what is going to happen, we sometimes fear the worst, including our own death. Autopilot tends to make up stories to fill in what we don't know. This is a survival mechanism. By generating and thinking about what might happen, we can prepare for various scenarios. Such thinking can be helpful if it is done as a conscious decision to plan for possibilities in the future. However, more often it takes the form of worry, with the mind going in circles in habitual thinking ruts. Through mindfulness, you can learn to relax with not knowing. Perhaps you can shift perspective and see uncertainty as exciting rather than scary.

Avoidance and Suffering

Mindfulness teaches us that resisting physical or emotional pain results in suffering. Amy's worry and anxiety were causing her to suffer on a daily basis, and were doing nothing to actually prevent the pain she would feel when her mother passed away. She was resisting what she could not control—in this case, the fact that all of us will die one day. Amy realized that her path to being free from anxiety was to be fully present with her fear. She started by working on being present with her physical symptoms of anxiety, as you will learn to do in the following pages. She found that most of the time, the anxiety would fade away quickly when she was able to relax with the sensations. Of course, it took some practice for her to be able to do this.

Eventually, by practicing meditation focused on the reality that her mother would eventually die, Amy found that she could be at peace with that. More importantly, she experienced the pain of that truth and found it was bearable. By being present with and accepting of reality, she was able to stop resisting. Her anxiety improved dramatically.

You too can learn how to stay present with difficult emotions like anxiety and worry. The next section will present a meditation to help you focus on these unpleasant emotions.

Being Present with Anxiety

Anxiety is an excessive fear response. The fear is either excessive for the situation or completely unnecessary. Sometimes it may be tied to a specific situation, as it was for Amy, or it may just come on out of the blue. Although anxiety can feel really awful, it's not dangerous. Most importantly, like all thoughts and emotions, it will pass. Mindfulness teaches us that nothing is permanent.

The key to liberation from suffering is to be able to be present with the reality of the moment, whether it is pleasant, unpleasant, or neutral. Trying to resist always makes things worse. This is true if the resistance is to a specific situation, as in Amy's case, or if it's to an unpleasant emotion. Of course, this doesn't mean that you shouldn't take appropriate action to change things that can be changed. But the first step is to be present with the reality of the moment so that you don't get caught up in autopilot. If reality is painful, then you have to experience that pain.

Mindfulness can completely change your perception of anxiety and other symptoms. Before practicing mindfulness, Amy feared her anxiety and always wanted it to go away. After she learned that the way out of anxiety was to be present with it, she almost welcomed it when it came on. For her, having anxiety was like going to the gym for a workout. Every time she had the opportunity to practice with anxiety, she got stronger. Every bout of anxiety was a chance to strengthen her mindfulness muscle. What a change in perspective! You too can have that shift in how you think about your symptoms. And this shift will change your life.

The practice you are about to learn will help you with the mindful minute that you learned in the last chapter. As you remember, the goal of the mindful minute is to help you move out of autopilot thinking and emotional patterns and into mindful awareness of the present moment. However, if you use the mindful minute when you are experiencing distressing symptoms or feeling very stressed—which is definitely when you want to use it—you will likely notice that there is a strong tendency to fall back into autopilot. Your mind desperately wants to avoid the pain that distress causes. Again, it's a reflex, like jerking your hand away from a hot burner. But to get out of autopilot, you have to stay with the reality of the moment, even if it's painful.

This next practice will help you stay in the moment. Remember that once you see things clearly from the viewpoint of mindful awareness, you often will see actions that you can take to feel better.

Sitting Meditation with Focus on an Unpleasant Emotion

In this meditation you will intentionally hold an unpleasant emotion in your awareness. The emotion you will focus on here is anxiety, but later you can practice with other uncomfortable emotions. To practice this meditation, you should be sitting as you would for any sitting meditation in a space that will provide few distractions (see chapter 4). Read through the instructions and then do the meditation. A guided audio version of this meditation is also available online: visit http://www.newharbinger.com/31854 to access it.

Getting ready: *Think of something that causes you anxiety or fear. Decide on what you will use before you start to meditate. Think of something that brings on a degree of anxiety that isn't overwhelming—maybe a level of two or three on a scale of one to ten, where one represents hardly any feeling, and ten the worst feeling of anxiety and fear. For example, if flying sometimes makes you anxious, you may think of flying with some turbulence. But if flying always makes you anxious, you may choose to think just about going to the airport. Before starting the meditation, you may want to experiment a little to find something that kicks up some mild anxiety that you can feel in your body. If you notice a little tightening of your chest or tensing of your muscles, then that should be about right.*

Starting the meditation: *The meditation is very simple. Begin with the sitting meditation with focus on the breath (see chapter 4). Start out as you have been practicing it on a daily basis. Sit for about five minutes with your attention focused on your breath. Then bring the anxiety-provoking situation into your awareness. Imagine an open space in your awareness where the situation can be present. Start by holding it there in your awareness. Aim to keep your attention on the situation for about five minutes. Keep some of your attention on your breath to stay anchored in the present moment.*

Watching what happens: *The important part of this meditation is what happens while you are holding the anxiety-provoking situation in your awareness. Try to notice everything that happens in your mind and in your body. This is the key to your recovery—the ability to stay mindfully aware of what is happening, moment by moment, as you are experiencing symptoms. This is the only way to avoid the autopilot responses that make symptoms worse.*

Observing your thoughts: *Pay close attention to your thoughts while you are focusing on the anxiety-causing situation. First, notice what the situation looks like in your mind's eye. Is there an image? Is it a series of thoughts? What happens over time? Does the situation stay sharp in your awareness, or does it get fuzzy and indistinct? Is it hard to keep it in your awareness? What thoughts arise in response to the situation? Do you notice any habitual autopilot thinking patterns? Pay close attention to what happens to your thoughts as you observe them. Notice if your autopilot thinking patterns keep spinning in your head or if they dwindle away. Remember that you don't have to do anything with them. Stay in the present moment by keeping some of your attention on your breath. When you notice that you are getting carried away with* autopilot—just gently escort your attention back to the breath and to the present moment. Again, it's the ability to notice when you are on autopilot and then move yourself back to mindful awareness that is critical for your practice. The more you get to practice that, the easier it will become. The more your mind wanders during meditation, the more you benefit!

Being aware of body sensations: Along with watching your thoughts, pay close attention to what arises in your body. For example, you might notice a feeling of tightness in your chest or other sensations. Notice how you are breathing. Whatever you feel is your reality. You might not feel anything. That's okay. Reality is just reality. It is whatever it is. If you do feel body sensations of anxiety, explore them with an attitude of curiosity and acceptance. Try to learn as much as you can. If you feel tightness in your chest, notice exactly where it is located. Notice if the tightness stays in the same area or moves. Try to describe to yourself exactly what the feelings are like. Burning? Pressured? Tingling? Notice how this experience may be very different from your usual relationship with symptoms of anxiety. Most people usually want to get rid of the physical sensations of anxiety, but after starting their mindfulness practice, they become more curious about these sensations.

Watching anxiety fade: Sometimes anxiety may fade quickly, and other times it may persist. Be careful that you don't hold on to a preference for it to go away. If at some level your autopilot still wants the anxiety to go away, it probably won't. Discover what happens in your body.

Ending the meditation: Bring your meditation to an end by focusing all of your attention on the breath for a minute or two.

Take a few minutes after finishing the meditation to think about what you have learned. What autopilot scripts did you find? Did they tend to stick around once you found them, or did they fade away?

When Amy used this meditation to work with her fears around losing her mother, she discovered several autopilot scripts. One was that she should be able to prevent her mother's death. She also noticed a recurrent thought that she would not be able to survive the pain of grieving her mother's death. As she observed her scripts and noticed their irrationality, they tended to fade away. What happened in your case?

Autopilot scripts can go away, as they did in Amy's case, but more often they can be persistent. Most people find that one script leads to another and then to another, and so on. Again, it's important not to judge what's going on but to let your thoughts just be.

How did anxiety manifest in your mind and body? What did you learn?

When Amy did this meditation, she discovered that her muscles became tight and that she started breathing more quickly. She also noticed a heavy feeling in her chest. These physical sensations of anxiety usually dissipated quickly. Amy was surprised to find out that if she invited the feared situation to be present, it actually tended to wither away. It was difficult to keep in her awareness. She also discovered that the emotions associated with her fear were not that hard to tolerate. She didn't like the way she felt, but it wasn't overwhelming. Amy found the practice to be very freeing. How about you?

After Your Meditation

Be kind to yourself. You just did something that required some courage. You may want to take a few minutes now to do something that you enjoy. Through mindfulness, you can start to notice when you need to give yourself some nurturing. Now may be one of those times. In fact, whenever you do this meditation or the mindful minute, you can take a few minutes afterward to do something nice for yourself. One of the goals of mindfulness is to become aware that we need to show compassion for ourselves.

Remember that the goal of this meditation is not to make you feel bad. The aim is to decrease your suffering from the symptoms of bipolar disorder. You can do that by learning to be fully present with whatever symptoms exist in the moment. This is essential to avoid the trap of autopilot thinking. Once you can see things clearly from the perspective of mindful awareness, the next step is to take any actions that may help you feel better.

Keeping Up Your Practice

The meditation you learned in this chapter is probably the most important for your recovery. I recommend practicing it at least once a day. Try it with any symptoms of bipolar disorder that you experience. Use it with your lower-level symptoms for the first few weeks, and then gradually increase the intensity of the symptoms that you practice with. Examples of lower-level symptoms include mild symptoms of anxiety (the practice you just completed) as well as sadness, irritability, and agitation. As you develop this skill, you can start working with more intense and complex symptoms too. Note that as you begin to work with more challenging symptoms, you may find it more difficult to avoid going on autopilot. While you may find this frustrating, encountering this resistance will actually strengthen your practice. With time, you will discover that you don't have to fear any symptoms of bipolar disorder. That realization is your path to recovery.

chapter 7

observing your
thinking patterns

One of the things that you will discover with practicing mindfulness regularly is that you have a voice in your head. That voice is your thoughts. Your thoughts can include images, but the voice is the primary way you experience your thoughts. Another thing you will learn from mindfulness is that the voice rarely shuts up. It goes on and on whenever you are awake. Finally, by being mindfully aware of your thoughts, you can see that they are often illogical and frequently repeat the same thing over and over. That's why many meditation traditions call this phenomenon monkey mind. The mind's always up there chattering away. In mindfulness language, this is the same as autopilot.

In previous chapters, you have seen how your thoughts can contribute to the symptoms of bipolar disorder. This chapter will look more deeply into how thinking patterns cause emotional distress and unhappiness. One of the main goals of a mindfulness practice is to develop a new relationship with your thoughts. In this chapter, you will learn how to do that.

How Automatic Thinking Patterns Develop

We all have autopilot thinking patterns that serve us poorly. These develop as a result of our life experiences and learning. Some of the most powerful thinking ruts develop because of painful events that have occurred in our lives. One of autopilot's jobs is to protect us. So when we experience pain, autopilot will try to keep us from getting hurt again. When we have a bad experience, we think twice before getting ourselves into the same situation again. This is often a good thing. But sometimes the thinking patterns are so strong that they keep us from taking any risks at all. As a result, we become stuck in certain areas of our lives, such as romantic relationships. Tom's story is a good illustration of how this can happen.

• Tom's Story

Tom started practicing mindfulness to work with ruminative thinking patterns that were making his bipolar depression worse. As he was able to become an observer of his thoughts using mindful awareness, he began to notice specific thinking patterns that tended to come up time after time. In particular, he noticed that he tended to think in a specific way in response to certain situations. Tom noticed that he would get stuck in autopilot thinking ruts.

One thinking pattern that was contributing to Tom's depression came up in response to potential romantic relationships. Tom knew that he wanted to find a partner, but every time he met someone he was interested in, he found that he was unable to start a relationship. He had no problem with going on a first date, but if it went well, then he would be reluctant to get together again. By watching his thoughts, Tom began to see that he would always find a problem with the other person. Tom had been aware of this kind of thinking before practicing mindfulness, but his perspective changed as his practice deepened. He started to see his thinking as being autopilot based and frequently illogical. Tom realized that anyone he dated would have some traits and behaviors that he didn't like. He became aware that his thinking patterns were blowing minor things out of proportion and keeping him from having the relationship he wanted. He discovered that it was not only his lack of an intimate partner but also his ruminating about the imperfections of others that contributed to his depression.

At times, having protective thoughts—such as, *I was really hurt by that breakup, and I'm never going to date again*—can be very straightforward. But protective thinking also can be disguised, as it was in Tom's case. His constant finding of imperfections in potential partners was really an attempt by autopilot to keep Tom from being hurt. In his work with a psychotherapist, he discovered that the loss of his mother at a young age had been traumatic, and he was very afraid of being hurt like that again. Autopilot's solution was to protect him by always finding an insurmountable problem with any new relationship.

All of us have autopilot thinking patterns that have developed over the years of our lives. Some of those patterns are helpful and some are not. Through mindfulness, we can begin to see which ones are and which ones aren't. The most important point is to recognize that our irrational and unhelpful thinking isn't something we signed up for. We didn't decide to think irrationally. The thinking errors developed as a result of our experiences and are often autopilot's attempt to protect us from being hurt. We need to have compassion for ourselves and for our autopilot habits when we notice problems with our thinking patterns. Autopilot is just trying to do its job.

How to Recognize Bipolar Autopilot Scripts

By becoming an observer of your own thoughts, you can see the scripts that tend to play over and over in your head. Your task is to see which scripts contribute to your symptoms of bipolar disorder.

Two Types of Scripts

Some scripts may be very specific to symptoms, like John's bipolar depressive thinking patterns, described in chapter 5. Other scripts may be related to life situations, like Tom's autopilot thinking patterns or Amy's thinking patterns (see chapter 6). Even though Tom's and Amy's autopilot scripts are not specifically about their bipolar symptoms, both discovered that getting stuck in their habitual thinking ruts made their symptoms worse.

It would seem as if once you became aware of the concept of autopilot, it would be easy to see how it impacts your day-to-day life. Unfortunately, this is not the case. The problem is that we tend to get carried away by our thoughts. When caught up in autopilot thinking, we don't recognize it as autopilot and usually don't see that it is our thoughts that are causing our distress. This is why it is essential for you to practice mindfulness meditation on a daily basis. By practicing, you train your mindfulness muscle to become stronger. Eventually, you will be able to see when you are on autopilot even when you are not practicing formal meditation. Then you can use the mindful minute from chapter 5 to pull yourself out of autopilot and into the present moment.

Checking In with Yourself

You are most likely to be on autopilot when experiencing unpleasant emotions, such as depression, sadness, anxiety, or anger. Whenever you notice that you are not feeling good emotionally, check to see if you are on autopilot. Use the mindful minute to move into mindful awareness. Then notice what autopilot scripts were running in your head while you were upset. It may be helpful to keep a journal in which to write these scripts down. Your goal is to find out what autopilot scripts contribute to your symptoms.

Again, often autopilot is trying to help by attempting either to prevent or to get rid of emotional or physical pain. Your job is to find out which autopilot thinking patterns are helpful and which ones aren't. You must discover for yourself whether you can think unpleasant emotions away. If you find that you have thinking patterns that help you feel better, then by all means use them. Most of us, however, find that we cannot get rid of emotional pain by just thinking. What we can do is be fully present with the pain so that it can pass.

Doing a Reality Check

Another problem with autopilot is that it is usually biased thinking, because we tend to see life from our own unique viewpoint. That isn't good or bad; it's just the reality of how the mind works. For example, Tom's view of reality around relationships was obscured by his autopilot thinking patterns that always found insurmountable problems with anyone he started to date. Once he was able to see that his thinking wasn't reality based, he could avoid being carried away with those thoughts. This has changed Tom's life. He has now been dating someone for about six months and they are talking about getting engaged. Seeing your day-to-day reality more clearly can profoundly change your life too.

As you observe your thoughts, notice how your habitual thinking patterns often aren't consistent with reality. Our minds tend to generate thoughts to fill in gaps in our knowledge. For example, if a friend is short with us on the phone, we may spend minutes or hours generating scenarios, thinking, *What did I do wrong?* or *Is she still upset about what happened last week?* or *I'll bet he's mad because I forgot...*you get the picture. We all do this. The problem is that while we are running these scenarios through our heads, they feel real. Usually this ruminating makes us feel bad, and often it may have little to do with reality. For example, the friend may have been only in a hurry and not upset with us at all. But these made-up scenarios also distort how we think about our friend. For example, until we find out the truth, we may think our friend was being mean when, in fact, she was feeling rushed and distracted. Often, we never find out the truth and go on with a false idea stuck in our heads.

The bottom line is that, at best, our thoughts are usually only partially correct, because we can never see the entire picture. Often our view is obscured by long-term habitual thinking errors, as was the case for Tom, or short-term thinking patterns like the one just described.

Seeing Thoughts as Just Thoughts

Now that you know that you can't really trust your thoughts, what do you do? Just having this knowledge will help you begin to take your thinking patterns less seriously and to expect that what you think may be wrong. However, the most important thing is to develop a different relationship with your thoughts.

So, what kind of relationship with your thoughts should you have? The answer is a relationship in which you see your thoughts as just thoughts and nothing more. Because our thoughts are the mechanism by which we understand the world and ourselves, we tend to see them as representing some profound truth about life and who we are. But thoughts are just language happening in our heads. We can call a chair a chair, but the language we use isn't the chair, whether we say the word out loud or just think it. Our thoughts are not who we are. Or to put it the other way around, we are not our thoughts. Thoughts provide a mechanism to think about who we are, but they are not our essence.

My meditation teacher often says, "The stomach secretes acid and the brain secretes thoughts. Both have the same degree of meaning." Both can be helpful, but neither stomach acid nor our thoughts represent the core of our being.

The kind of relationship with your thoughts that you want to have is to appreciate them as just thoughts. However, hearing that thoughts are just thoughts won't change your relationship with your own autopilot. You have to observe your own thoughts until you are convinced beyond a shadow of a doubt that your thoughts are just thoughts. They arise and pass, like everything in life. You do not have to cling to them; you can just let them come and go.

Suppressing Thoughts Doesn't Work

You might get the idea that you should try to get rid of your autopilot thinking. This goes along with another idea that some people have about meditation—that their mind should be quiet. Neither idea is correct from a mindfulness perspective.

Mindfulness is about being fully present with reality, whatever it may be in the moment. If you are meditating and your monkey mind is chattering, that is your reality at the time. With practice, you can develop a different relationship with autopilot so that you don't get carried away with it but let it run like a TV in the background. You may still be thinking, *But why not just try to get rid of autopilot?* Part of the answer is that sometimes autopilot can be helpful for us. For example, many things that we do automatically, like driving a car or brushing your teeth, allow us to be efficient. Some thinking patterns are helpful too, such as using learned knowledge to solve problems. Through mindfulness, we develop the skill to determine whether any given autopilot pattern is helpful or not—in the present moment. The other part is that suppressing autopilot, or thoughts in general, doesn't work. It's like playing whack-a-mole—if you smack a thought down, it will pop back up again. In mindfulness, you accept autopilot as reality but observe it rather than get caught up in the drama.

Thoughts Are Neither Good nor Bad

You want to be able to recognize when your thinking patterns are unhelpful. At the same time, it's important to avoid labeling general thinking patterns and individual thoughts as either good or bad. Labeling your thoughts in this way is not recommended from a mindfulness perspective.

What's the difference between recognizing that a thinking pattern is unhelpful and labeling it as bad? There is a subtle but important distinction. For one thing, we usually want to get rid of things that we think are bad, but the aim is not to get rid of autopilot thinking. More importantly, labeling your thoughts as bad or good may start another string of autopilot thoughts, such as *Why am I thinking this way? I shouldn't be having these thoughts.* You get the idea. In contrast, the act of recognizing that a thought is or isn't helpful right now is much more neutral. It's like looking in your toolbox and seeing a hammer when you know what you need is a screwdriver. There is no need to judge the hammer or to do anything about it. Similarly, with unhelpful thoughts, you just notice that they're there and move on. You let them be. That's what you want to do with autopilot.

Seeing Yourself on Autopilot

One of the main goals of a mindfulness practice is to recognize how much we are driven by autopilot. We do that by learning to see autopilot during our regular meditation practice. That is the purpose of the meditation that you will learn in this chapter. Then we extend mindfulness into our day-to-day lives so that we can fully appreciate the extent to which we are driven by automatic thinking and behavior patterns.

As you develop this skill, you may be surprised to discover how much of your life is lived on autopilot. Be careful not to make judgments about that, either. It is the reality for all of us. You also will likely start to recognize autopilot-driven thoughts, emotions, and behaviors after—rather than before—they occur. This too is to be expected. Please avoid criticizing yourself for not recognizing what was going on before it happened. It may be particularly difficult when autopilot leads you to act in ways that you later regret. As your practice develops, you will gain the skill to start recognizing autopilot when it's happening. Doing this takes practice, however, and none of us will ever be perfect at it. Plus, the stronger your emotions are in the moment, the less likely you are to see that you are on autopilot. But the longer you practice and the more time you spend practicing every week, the better you will become at recognizing autopilot when it starts.

You can use this next meditation to change your relationship with your thoughts. This is how you come to see monkey mind for what it is.

Sitting Meditation While Watching Thoughts

Approach this meditation like a scientific experiment, in which you test a hypothesis—in this case, the theory that thoughts are insubstantial, without deep meaning, and that they are often inaccurate and misleading. The experiment is just to watch the thoughts and see what you discover. To practice, you should sit as you would for any sitting meditation—in a comfortable space with few distractions. Read through the instructions and then do the meditation. A guided audio version of this meditation is also available online: visit http://www.newharbinger.com/31854 to access it.

Getting started: *Begin this meditation just as you did the sitting meditation with focus on the breath in chapter 4. Sit with your attention focused on the present moment by anchoring your concentration on the breath for about three minutes. As always, whenever your attention wanders, gently escort it back to the breath. Don't try to suppress your thoughts, but just let them run freely in the background.*

Expanding your awareness: *Now expand your awareness to include the physical sensations of your body and the sounds around you. Notice that these sounds and sensations arise and pass. Let them just come and go without clinging on to them. Keep your awareness on the breath, body sensations, and sounds for about three minutes. If you notice that you are carried away with thoughts, just move your attention back to the present moment anchored by the sounds around you, your sensations, and your breath.*

Watching your thoughts: *To observe your thoughts, imagine creating a spacious, open area in your mind. You might imagine yourself reclining on your back in the grass on a summer day and looking up at the sky with clouds floating by. The place in your mind is like the sky, where thoughts can arise and pass like clouds. The clouds don't disturb the sky; it remains peaceful as they come and go. Similarly, thoughts don't disturb your mind when you observe them in mindful awareness; they just arise and pass.*

Relaxing in mindful awareness: *You may find that thoughts don't come up while you are watching for them. If so, that's okay. Just be present with spacious, open awareness. Or you may have lots of thoughts and get carried away with them at times. That's okay too; just notice when it happens and direct your attention back to mindful awareness. You may find it helpful to say to yourself, I'm having a lot of thoughts right now. You can name the topic of your thoughts, but avoid the tendency to label these thoughts as good or bad.*

Ending the meditation: *Continue this meditation for three to five minutes, and then bring the meditation to an end by contracting your awareness to focus on the breath for a minute or two.*

After doing the meditation, think about what you learned from your experiment. Consider making notes about it, perhaps in a journal. Were you able to see the insubstantial nature of your thoughts? Did you notice any habitual thinking patterns or autopilot scripts? Did you often get carried away with thoughts?

Getting carried away with thoughts happens to all of us, no matter how much we practice meditation. Again, please avoid making judgments when this happens to you, and avoid labeling a meditation session as good or bad, depending upon how often you were carried away with your thoughts. From a mindfulness viewpoint, there is no need to do that. We just recognize that reality was reality. If you were carried away with your thoughts, you were carried away with your thoughts. Recognizing how easily you can be carried away with monkey mind is also an important part of meditation practice. It helps you understand the nature of the mind and to see clearly how autopilot drives your behaviors. Finally, the more often you recognize you are on autopilot and move your attention back to the present moment, the more you strengthen your meditation muscle.

Doing this meditation regularly will help. Try doing it at least three times per week. You can do it every day, if you want, as part of your regular practice.

Mindfulness in Your Everyday Bipolar Life

Your mindfulness practice is now off to a good start. You have a daily practice going, and you are using the mindful minute. Now you can make it an overarching goal to spend as much of your life as you can being as mindfully aware as you can—in other words, being fully present with your life, breath by breath and moment by moment. Of course, none of us will ever be fully present with every moment of our lives, because autopilot is just too powerful. But you can make it a goal to be in the present moment as much as possible. This is especially important for fostering your new relationship with your thoughts.

In addition to doing daily practice, you can approach any of your regular activities with mindful awareness. A formal meditation practice is how you train for this, just as an athlete trains in the gym; but the ultimate goal is to use your mindfulness skills in the game of life. A good start is to pick a regular activity and then try to do it mindfully each time you do it. This works best if it is a relatively short activity and if it is something that you do at least once a day, like brushing your teeth or combing your hair. Each time you do the activity, try to be fully present with the physical sensations involved. Notice that the tendency is to be on autopilot, thinking about the past or the future, and not paying any attention to what you are doing. When you find yourself going on autopilot, however, you can gently guide your attention back to what you are doing and let the thoughts run in the background. Some additional ideas for incorporating mindfulness into your daily life are in the appendix.

As your practice deepens, you will see more and more how autopilot runs your life. Autopilot can not only worsen your symptoms but also lead to unhappiness and dissatisfaction. Later chapters will talk more about that. For now, please try to watch your thoughts as much as you can. Extend the experiment to your entire life. Discover for yourself that thoughts are just thoughts.

chapter 8

working with mania and desire

This chapter focuses on the emotion of desire. As you know from your own experience, one symptom of mania and hypomania is an increased desire to experience pleasure. This desire can be intense and may lead to behaviors that are risky or that have potentially disastrous consequences. Mindfulness provides a way to be present with desire without having to act on it. This is a critical skill to have when you are bipolar.

Desire Is Almost Always with Us

We all experience desire on a daily basis. Desire is an awareness of wanting something that we don't currently have. Our desires can be big, such as for a new job or a new car, or small, like wanting a cup of coffee or needing to scratch an itch. Desire can be intense and overwhelming or just a slight preference for one thing over another. Such words as hunger or thirst describe specific desires. From a mindfulness perspective, it is important to recognize that desire, in one form or another, is almost always with us. Chapter 7 discussed the goal of staying mindfully aware throughout your daily life. As you spend more of your life with awareness focused on the present moment, please try to notice whenever desire arises. Most of us find that it is an almost constant companion.

Why We Need Desire

Scientists understand desire as the driving force that motivates living things to survive. In animals, this drive may be to do something very basic, such as eating and drinking. Of course, this is true for humans too. But for us, desire is also what motivates us to take the many complex actions that make us human. On an individual level, we educate ourselves, buy homes, get jobs, and have families. On a community level, we build buildings, bridges, and highways. We develop new technologies and invent things. We do all of this stuff because we have a desire for things to be different or better. This motivating force is necessary for our individual survival and for the survival of our species. It is also behind all the magnificent things we have accomplished as human beings. Desire plays a very big role in defining what it means to be a human. So, you can see desire is a wonderful emotion—except when it isn't.

Desire and Discontent

The other side of desire is that it underlies feelings of discontentment and dissatisfaction. One of the most important things that you learn from a mindfulness practice is that the mind is never satisfied for long. In particular, autopilot is never satisfied for long.

Our minds always want things to be different. We either want something that we don't currently have or want to get rid of something that we do have. Our autopilot scripts are often aimed at wanting things to be different from reality. In chapter 7, you met Tom, whose persistent discovery of imperfections in potential partners was an example of an autopilot-driven dissatisfaction. Or to put it another way, Tom had an unrealistic, autopilot-based desire for perfection in women he dated. Because the desire could never be satisfied, he experienced persistent dissatisfaction in his romantic relationships. Tom's experience is an example of a very specific life situation. However, all of us experience on a daily basis the mind's tendency to be dissatisfied.

As your mindfulness practice develops, please notice when desire and dissatisfaction arise in your daily life. Most of us discover that these emotions can be intense at times and much more subtle at others. Subtle examples can include our many preferences, which are desires for things to be a certain way. We might have a preference for sunny days over cloudy days or for our food to be prepared a certain way. Through mindful awareness, you will discover that you have preferences for almost everything that you encounter— music, people, clothing, you name it. This isn't a bad thing. It is part of what defines who you are as a person. However, please notice that the more tightly we cling to our preferences, the more we will experience dissatisfaction, because the universe rarely gives us exactly what we want.

At another level, our minds usually don't feel satisfied for long after our desire is fulfilled. Amy, whom you met in chapter 6, bought a new car last year. By practicing mindfulness, she was able to see that although she really liked having her new car, she soon started wanting something else. As her practice has deepened, she has realized that feelings of satisfaction are fleeting and that there is always something else for her mind to desire. For a while, Amy thought this happened just for material things like a new car. Then she finished school and started working for a nonprofit organization that helps underprivileged children. She found the work very meaningful but was surprised to discover that after a while she started feeling like her work didn't completely satisfy her. She had a vague sense that there should be something more. By watching her own mind, she can now see this is just her mind's autopilot desire that never feels completely satisfied.

Recognizing that the mind tends to be dissatisfied is key to living with the symptoms of bipolar disorder as well as to finding happiness and joy in life. We discover that we can let the sense of dissatisfaction run in the background without needing to respond to it and, at the same time, experience the joy of being alive in the moment.

Being Present with Excessive Desire

Before Amy's mood symptoms were treated, she experienced episodes of mania and milder episodes of hypomania. Like most people with bipolar disorder, she experienced intense desire for pleasure during these episodes. The strongest craving was for sexual gratification, but she also experienced a strong desire to buy clothes and fashion accessories. These cravings were so powerful and persistent that she often engaged in risky sexual behaviors and spent excessive amounts of money. Needless to say, these behaviors created serious problems in her life.

Amy's mood symptoms are under generally good control now, but she still experiences mild episodes of hypomanic symptoms that can last for several days. During these episodes, she typically notices an increase in energy, mild euphoria, and a desire to shop and spend money. Amy has found that her mindfulness practice has helped her work with that desire in a way that helps her avoid excessive spending.

Amy has discovered the power in the mindfulness practice of being present with desire. By sitting in mindfulness meditation with desire, Amy is able to see her desires as just passing thoughts and sensations. Rather than getting carried away with the feelings, she is able to sit and watch them arise and pass. Instead of feeling the need to satisfy the compulsion to spend and buy, she simply can observe the sensations of desire. By closely examining her desire, she can see it as just a passing thought with no substance. She also can see that if she were to buy a new outfit, her mind would not be satisfied for long, and soon she would want something else. Through meditation, Amy doesn't try to make the desire go away. Rather, by sitting with her desire, she can see it for what it really is. You can do this too.

Desire as Empty of Substance

Mindfulness teaches us that all thoughts and feelings are transitory and insubstantial. This is also true for the emotion of desire. As your mindfulness practice deepens, try to see desire as it really is. The fundamental misunderstanding that we have about desire is that we think that by satisfying our wants, we will experience happiness and joy. Satisfying desire may lead to a short-term experience of pleasure, but it will never take us to true happiness, because the mind will become dissatisfied and want something else. The pathway to genuine joy is to be fully present with each moment.

Freedom to Choose

We practice mindfulness to experience freedom from suffering. Mindfulness also gives us the freedom to choose. Because autopilot is so strong and because we often don't recognize it, our behaviors are very frequently driven by it. This is especially true during manic or hypomanic mood episodes, as Amy's story illustrates.

Mindful awareness allows us to see reality clearly. We can see circumstances without having our vision clouded by autopilot-based thoughts and emotions. We can see that satisfying a desire may lead to short-term pleasure but not long-term happiness. We also can see if there will be positive or negative consequences from satisfying the desire. Then we get to choose.

Sitting Meditation Being Present with Desire

This meditation is very similar to the meditation that you did in chapter 6; however, instead of focusing on an unpleasant emotion, you will focus on staying present with desire. Read through the instructions and then do the meditation. A guided audio version of this meditation is also available online; visit at http://www.newharbinger.com/31854 to access it.

Getting ready: *Prepare by thinking of something that causes a sensation of desire. Pick something with about a level of two or three on a scale of one to ten, where one represents hardly any desire and ten the greatest desire. In other words, choose* *something that brings up some desire but isn't overwhelming. For example, if you like chocolate, imagine a piece of your favorite kind and how good it would taste to eat it.*

Overview of the meditation: *Start with the sitting meditation focusing on the breath (see chapter 4). First, sit with your attention focused on your breath. Then, expand your awareness to include all of the physical sensations in your body, including the breath. Pay attention to all the subtle body sensations that you are not normally conscious of. Notice if your muscles are tense or relaxed. Finally, expand your awareness again to include the sounds you can hear. Now, bring the desire-provoking situation into your awareness. Imagine an open space in your awareness where the situation can be present. Aim to keep your attention on the situation for about five minutes. It may be helpful to keep some of your attention on your breath to stay anchored in the present moment. Notice what arises within you in response to desire. Do habitual thinking patterns start running through your head? Notice in particular if there are thoughts about how good it would feel to satisfy the desire. Is there a belief that if the desire were satisfied, that moment would be preferable to the present moment? Also, try to discover if there is any response in your body. Just notice what happens without judgment.*

Ending the meditation: *Bring the meditation to an end by focusing all of your attention on the breath for a minute or two.*

Spend a few minutes after finishing the meditation to think about what you have learned. Did desire cause any physical sensations in your body? What thoughts came up? Did you notice any autopilot thinking patterns? Most importantly, were you able to see the transient and insubstantial nature of desire?

Practice this meditation several times each week as part of your regular practice. Notice if your relationship to desire changes over time.

Encountering Barriers

How is your mindfulness practice going so far? Have you discovered any challenges or barriers that interfere with your practice? Most of us do. Practicing meditation on a daily basis is a major commitment. There are bound to be some difficulties.

From a mindfulness perspective, the impediments to practicing are just reality as it is in our lives. We acknowledge the obstructions, and we practice anyway. Most importantly, we recognize that our mindfulness practice—like life—will be imperfect. Most of us feel that we don't find time to practice as often as we want or as we think we should. The main thing is not to give up. Just do the best you can. Really that is all any of us can ever do.

If you haven't done so yet, now might be a good time to see if there are any meditation groups or classes in your community that you can practice with. Practicing with others, at least occasionally, can be really helpful.

chapter 9

---

managing irritability and anger

Aversion is a feeling of dislike, distaste, or repulsion toward something. Aversion and anger go together because both emotions come up in response to persons, events, or situations that we don't like. The emotion of anger can feel scary because it is often very intense and may make you feel out of control. Anger goes by many names, including irritation, impatience, fury, and resentment. It can range in intensity from mild annoyance to full-blown rage. Irritability is the tendency to feel excessive anger and frustration and is common with episodes of both depression and mania. In this chapter, you will learn to develop a new relationship with aversion, anger, and irritability.

Having Something You Don't Want

If desire is our wanting something that we don't have (see chapter 8), then aversion, anger, and irritability are the opposite of this. These emotions come up when we don't want something that we do have. You may not typically think of these feelings in that way; but to understand this from a mindfulness perspective, it is helpful to contemplate how the mind is rarely satisfied and almost always wants things to be different from how they are. That is, our minds tend to want things we don't have (desire) or want to get rid of things that we do have (aversion and anger). Examples of things we might have and want to get rid of can include illnesses, pain, financial problems, relationship difficulties, or anything that is stressful or unpleasant in our lives. When we have something that we don't want, we may experience aversion or anger, or both.

From a mindfulness viewpoint, we don't need to label aversion and anger as good or bad emotions—they just exist. The same is true for irritability. In fact, all of these emotions can be very useful at times. For example, aversion can motivate us to avoid things that may not be good for us. A simple example would be eating a piece of rotten food. When we see and smell it, we feel disgust or repulsion. The main purpose of anger is to give us the energy to protect others or ourselves from harm. Without anger, we might not stand up for others or for ourselves when we need to.

However, as with desire, these feelings can drive our unhappiness and sense of dissatisfaction, because the mind is never satisfied. Once we get rid of something we don't like, something else will come along that we dislike or that annoys us or makes us angry.

The key is to learn to be present with these emotions and, in doing so, to form a different relationship with them. As discussed throughout this book, mindfulness is simply staying present with reality, as it exists in each moment. We do that so that we don't get caught up and carried away by autopilot-based thoughts, emotions, and behaviors. We don't suppress these thoughts and emotions; we let them just run in the background while we keep our attention focused on the present moment. The aim is to develop a different relationship with our autopilot thinking, so that we can watch the river of our thoughts and feelings flow by rather than allow ourselves to be carried away in the flood.

• *Alex's Story*

Alex has bipolar II disorder, and his hypomanic and depressive episodes both tend to be irritable. His experience of the irritability was very negative. He didn't like feeling that way. Because of experiencing so much irritability in his life, he became very uncomfortable with the emotions of aversion and anger. By practicing mindfulness, however, he was able to see that he often tried to avoid experiencing these feelings. He also discovered that suppressing his anger often inhibited his ability to respond appropriately to situations when he needed to be more assertive.

As his mindfulness practice has deepened, Alex has found that he is more able to stay present with anger and to harness it to give him the energy to take constructive action in difficult situations. He also has found that by experiencing aversion more fully, he has become more aware of his likes and dislikes. He understands himself better. Alex was really surprised to discover that even his irritability could be useful. He found that it gave him important information about when he was getting stressed or needed to evaluate his life to make a change.

The take-home message is that as with all emotions, aversion and anger are necessary, and they can help us navigate the difficulties of life. However, because our minds are never satisfied, we will tend to continually experience dislike, annoyance, and frustration because the universe isn't the way that we want it to be.

Aversion and Desire in Bipolar Disorder

The autopilot thoughts and emotions that tend to cause the most problems in bipolar disorder can be grouped into the two general categories of desire and aversion. The desire group includes craving, longing, hunger, thirst, and passion. Aversion includes the feelings of anger, annoyance, resentment, bitterness, and irritability. Put another way, desire and aversion are the same as our mind's autopilot *wanting* and *not wanting*. They are flipsides of the same autopilot thinking, as Alex began to realize in his mindfulness practice.

Alex came to see his mood episodes much more clearly as he continued to practice mindfulness. Rather than being carried away by depression and hypomania, he was able to observe what was really going on in his mind. During depressive episodes, he found that what he experienced was mostly excessive aversion. This took the form of not liking much of anything in his life and particularly disliking the way he was feeling emotionally. However, Alex was surprised to find some elevated desire as well while he was depressed. He found that he wanted to sleep more and had intense cravings for certain foods. In contrast, his hypomania was more associated with desire, but he was usually also very irritable.

By staying fully present with his mood episodes, Alex found out that most of his symptoms consisted of autopilot-based thoughts and feelings of desire and aversion. He was able to see that both desire and aversion are transient and insubstantial. This allowed him to have a different relationship with his symptoms. His symptoms didn't go away, but they caused him much less distress and discomfort.

Alex found that even when he was *euthymic*, neither depressed nor manic, his mind was not satisfied. He often noticed autopilot-based thinking around desire and aversion. He clearly saw that this autopilot thinking was the source of most of his unhappiness and discontent in life. Though external life situations certainly contributed to his emotional state, it was his autopilot thinking (going over in his mind how he wanted things to be different from reality) that caused most of his sadness and dissatisfaction. He realized that the pathway to happiness and joy was simply to avoid being carried away with his desires and aversions. When he was able to do that and be fully present with each moment, he discovered that contentment and delight were already there waiting for him all along.

You Are Not Your Anger or Any Other Emotion

Mindfulness teaches us that we are not our thoughts and emotions. But what does this mean? Because we experience our thoughts and feelings intensely, we tend to feel that, to some degree, they define who we are as people. Before practicing mindfulness, for example, Alex thought of himself as an angry person. This caused him distress, because he didn't want to be that kind of person.

Do you have any labels for yourself based upon emotion? For example, you might think, *I'm a happy person*, or *I'm a sad person*, or maybe even *I'm an emotional person*.

In mindfulness, you shift perspective to realize that you are a person who experiences emotion. By watching thoughts and emotions, you see their transient and insubstantial nature. You see that they have no deep truth or meaning. They just arise and pass, as everything does. We experience thoughts and emotions, but they don't define us. Chapter 10 will continue to explore this concept. But first, it's time to make friends with your anger.

You can develop a new relationship with your anger. Perhaps you will discover, as Alex did, that anger can be very useful in your life. However, at another level, it's good to see that feelings of anger have no deep truth or meaning. Again, you can think of anger as being similar to stomach acid. Both serve a purpose, and too much of either can make you feel bad. Seeing anger as lacking any profound meaning can help you watch it come and go without being disturbed by it.

Sitting with Anger

The goal for this meditation is for you to develop a new relationship with the emotion of anger. Read through the instructions and then do the meditation. A guided audio version of this meditation is also available online at http://www.newharbinger.com/31854.

Getting ready: *Prepare by thinking of something that causes you to feel angry. Pick something with a level of two or three on a scale of one to ten, where one represents hardly any feeling and ten the strongest feeling of anger. In other words, choose something that brings up some frustration or annoyance but that doesn't bring on intense anger or rage.*

Overview of the meditation: *Start with the sitting meditation focusing on the breath that you learned in chapter 4. First, sit with your attention focused on your breath. Then expand your awareness to include all of the physical sensations in your body, including the breath. Finally, expand your awareness again to include the sounds that you can hear. Now bring the anger-provoking situation into your awareness. Imagine an open space in your awareness where the situation can be present. Keep your attention on the situation for about five minutes. It may be helpful to keep some of your attention on your breath to stay anchored in the present moment. As you have done with previous meditations, observe your own response without judgment. Notice how anger feels in your body. Notice if autopilot scripts start running through your head. Most importantly, see whether thoughts and emotions arise and pass. Do they sometimes come and go like clouds in the sky? Do your thoughts remind you of a monkey chattering?*

Ending the meditation: *Bring the meditation to an end by focusing all of your attention on the breath for a minute or two.*

Spend a few minutes after finishing the meditation to think about what you have learned. Did anger cause physical sensations in your body? What thoughts came up while you were experiencing anger? Were there any autopilot thinking patterns? Were you able to see the transient and insubstantial nature of anger?

Practice this meditation several times each week as part of your regular practice. Sometimes you may want to substitute situations that provoke more dislike or repulsion than anger.

Freedom from Fearing Your Symptoms

Mindfulness is about freedom. Freedom from suffering, freedom to make choices, and freedom from fear of your symptoms.

Do you fear your bipolar symptoms? Most people with bipolar disorder experience some fear of their symptoms, particularly depression. Depression feels awful. None of us wants to experience it. It is natural to feel fear toward it. Or maybe you haven't thought of your feelings as fear. Perhaps dread, apprehension, or trepidation are words that fit better for you. Maybe your anger feels scary. Most of us fear our anger or what we might do when angry.

Besides not feeling good, there is another major problem with fearing your symptoms: fear tends to make symptoms worse. Remember that autopilot is often aimed at protecting us. When we fear something, autopilot scripts kick in; and, as you have learned throughout this book, the autopilot cycle almost always makes symptoms worse rather than better.

Through practicing the meditations in this book, you have learned that you can be present with your symptoms. You practiced with depression in chapter 5, anxiety in chapter 6, desire in chapter 8, and anger in this chapter. By practicing mindfulness, you will discover that while you may not like the way your bipolar symptoms feel, they won't harm you. Most importantly, you will realize that you can tolerate them. You can go on with your life. This is the profound gift of mindfulness for bipolar disorder: you can let your symptoms run in the background and fully experience your life.

Welcoming Your Painful Symptoms

There's one more step that will help. The step, which I invite you to take, is to not only be present with your symptoms but also to actually welcome them.

Before you discard this idea as too off-the-wall, think about what you have learned so far from practicing mindfulness. You have learned that reality already exists and you can't change it. So, if you are feeling a symptom, such as the sadness of bipolar depression, it is already there whether you welcome it or not. You have nothing to lose by welcoming it. More importantly, you have learned that the more you allow your symptoms to be present, the more likely they are to fade away. Taking that a step further and welcoming them makes it even more likely that they will move along. An important point, though, is that it won't work if you welcome them with the ulterior motive of wanting them to go away.

At first this idea may be difficult to grasp. *How could I genuinely welcome my symptoms?* you may be thinking. Mindfulness helps you see that all you ever have is the present moment. Look for the past and future, and you won't find them. You can see evidence of the past, but you can't actually find some previous point in time. All you have is right now.

Through mindful awareness, then, you realize that each moment is precious, no matter what it holds. From that perspective, you can welcome whatever is in the moment, even your bipolar symptoms.

chapter 10

---

rethinking your bipolar self

This book has helped you focus on becoming mindfully aware of your thoughts and emotions. This chapter will explore more specifically how you think and feel about yourself. In particular, it will help you investigate autopilot-based thoughts and emotions that may define how you see yourself. It also will examine the concept of self in a more general way.

Bipolar Disorder and Self-Concept

Bipolar disorder causes distortions of self-concept, but keeping a mindfulness practice can help you correct those distortions. Alex, whom you met in chapter 9, has learned about this in his mindfulness practice over the last two years. By watching his thoughts, Alex has come to realize that the way that he sees himself depends on his mood. When depressed, he tends to see himself from a negative viewpoint. In contrast, when hypomanic, his view is excessively positive. He also has come to realize that the way he thinks in general about himself is mostly a result of habitual thinking patterns that developed when he was much younger—in other words, autopilot.

One of the main ways that practicing mindfulness can help you manage bipolar disorder is by helping you become more aware of your thinking patterns and emotional responses on a moment-by-moment basis. Through this process, you have discovered that your thoughts and emotions are just the firing of neurons and have no·deep truth or profound meaning. You have learned that autopilot-based thinking is often unhelpful and it frequently makes your bipolar symptoms worse. This is also true of thoughts and feelings about the self. Many of the thoughts that you have about yourself have very little basis in reality. This is true even for the memories of your life that you may feel define who you are as a person.

Alex realized this when he discovered the extent to which his self-concept changed with his mood state. During depressive episodes, he often thought of himself as not being very intelligent and as someone who was always making mistakes. When hypomanic, he tended to believe that he was one of the smartest people in the world and incapable of error. Finally, when in a euthymic mood state, Alex could see that in reality he was an intelligent and capable person. He also could recognize that, like everyone else, he sometimes made mistakes and that there were definitely people in the world with more intelligence than him.

Through his mindfulness practice, Alex was able to gain some distance from thoughts about himself and to not buy into them when depressed or hypomanic. This was very helpful for him, for during episodes of depression, he often would get caught up in a vicious cycle of having negative thoughts about himself, which led to more depression, which could lead to having an even darker view of himself, and so on. When hypomanic, his elevated self-esteem would cause him to do things that he later regretted. Observing his thinking patterns during mood episodes, rather than being carried away by them, helped Alex get better control of his illness. This can happen for you too.

Through mindfulness, you also may discover that the amount of time you spend thinking about yourself when you are experiencing symptoms is greater than usual. In other words, what changes is not only your thoughts but also the amount of time you spend thinking about yourself. This experience is common among people with bipolar disorder.

As you practice mindfulness, try to notice your habitual ways of thinking about yourself. Then observe how these may change with your mood state. See if you spend more time thinking about yourself during a mood episode. Whenever you discover that you are thinking excessively negative or positive thoughts about yourself, use the mindful minute from chapter 5 to move back into the present moment. From the clear perspective of mindfulness, you will be able to see your thinking as distorted. You will be able to let those thoughts just run in the background, where they won't disturb you, as you keep your attention focused on right now.

Exploring How You See Yourself

Gaining distance from the distorted thinking about the self that occurs during mood episodes can help you live well with bipolar disorder. However, a deeper exploration of how you see yourself can profoundly change your life.

As discussed in chapters 8 and 9, the mind is never satisfied for long. It tends either to want something you don't have or to want to get rid of, or escape from, something you do have. The mind also tends to be dissatisfied with the self, or how you think about yourself as a person. As you practice mindfulness, you will probably notice your thoughts manifesting both these tendencies.

How does your mind manifest discontent with the self? For Alex, it was often just a vague sense that his life should be different. Sometimes he thought that he should have chosen a different career, even though he was very successful in his work. At other times, he would be critical of how he looked, despite the fact that he was often complimented on his appearance. Most often he felt that he just wasn't living up to his full potential. Alex sometimes thought that having bipolar disorder meant he was deficient as a person in some way. Does having the illness of bipolar disorder bring up thoughts like this for you?

One day while sitting in meditation, Alex realized a fundamental truth—that no matter what he did or accomplished in his life, he would still feel a sense of dissatisfaction with himself. At that point, he fully understood the central concept of mindfulness, that his mind would never be satisfied for long about anything. At first, he found this realization depressing. It seemed most disheartening that he would never be totally happy with himself. After thinking about it for a few days, however, Alex had another revelation: knowing that he would never be completely satisfied actually freed him from his need to feel satisfied. He could just be himself and enjoy his life in each moment. He could be grateful for his life and the ability to be fully present with it. Alex also realized that even if he hadn't had bipolar disorder, he would experience a vague sense of being deficient. By practicing mindfulness, he could see that this dissatisfaction was autopilot thinking and had no real meaning. It was just monkey mind.

You too can be free from the need to respond to your mind's discontent. We will talk more about this in chapter 11, where you will learn more about how mindfulness can bring joy into your life.

Exploring Your Self

Through your mindfulness practice, you have discovered that the mind cannot be fully trusted. You can think of it as an infomercial playing in the background. Sometimes the programming contains useful information, but most of the time it is best not to pay too much attention to it.

What does this say about some of your deeply held beliefs? What about your deepest sense of who you are? Who are you, anyway? When you explore who you really are, you may be surprised by what you discover.

Alex was surprised when he explored this question. After realizing that his sense of discontent with himself and life was just his monkey mind chattering, he began to wonder about the beliefs and ideas he held about who he was. By sitting in meditation with these questions, he could see that he defined himself mostly through memories and autopilot-based thinking patterns. Thinking further about it, he realized that his memory of his life was very incomplete. Many key memories stuck out, but a lot of the day-to-day stuff had been forgotten.

He also noticed that many of the memories that seemed to define who he was were from negative experiences. For example, he had not been very athletic as a child and thus was always among the last to be picked to participate in games when he was in elementary school. Because of this, Alex saw himself as being clumsy and uncoordinated as an adult. He had always wanted to play softball in a local league but would never join a team, because he believed he wouldn't be able to play well. But after realizing that he'd been trapped by this autopilot-based thinking pattern, he had the courage to try out for a team. To his surprise, he was able to pick up the sport quickly and became a starting pitcher. Stepping out of autopilot-based thinking ruts about yourself can dramatically change your life.

Mindfulness can help you see that your self-concept is just a collection of thoughts and memories. Practicing can help you become less attached to these thoughts and memories and more fluid and flexible in your life. Like Alex, you can free yourself from autopilot-based definitions of who you are that are keeping you stuck. What thinking patterns and beliefs about yourself have ensnared you?

Letting Go of Habitual Thinking

Letting go of autopilot thinking about the self can be challenging. The mind will resist this because it can feel scary to have a less well-defined sense of self. As you practice letting go, notice if you experience resistance around doing this. While it may feel disconcerting to let go of strong beliefs about yourself, it isn't in any way dangerous. You will still be the same person—just a much freer and more flexible person.

Alex also discovered something else by practicing mindfulness. He found that his sense of being separate from others wasn't as strong as it had been. In other words, he felt more connected to other people and noticed that he was better able to take on viewpoints of others that were different from his own.

Shifting Your Perspective

We each tend to see the world from our own unique perspective, but mindfulness can help you shift your perspective away from this egocentric view of life. The word "egocentric" can bring up the notion of selfishness or being conceited or uncaring about others, but that's not the meaning here. Here it refers to the natural inclination of the mind to see the world from your own viewpoint. Having this egocentric view is not a bad thing. It's just the way all of our minds naturally work. In fact, this way of seeing the world is necessary for our survival—to get by in life, we have to be aware of and take care of our own needs. Again, I want to emphasize that this is very normal for all of us.

A problem with the egocentric viewpoint, however, is that it makes us feel very separate. But through mindfulness, we can become more flexible in how we see the world and life. We can become better able to take on the perspective of others.

Through mindfulness, you can become less attached to your own viewpoint. You can feel less separate and more connected to everyone around you. You can find that you are never alone, for in mindful awareness, you are always a part of something greater.

Accepting Yourself as You Are

The primary aim of this book is to help you live better with bipolar disorder. Another goal is to help you experience less suffering throughout your entire life. From the mindfulness perspective, suffering comes from wanting things to be different from how they are. The answer to suffering is to move into mindful awareness, where you can be fully present with reality without needing to fix or change it. From that perspective, you see that suffering comes from the autopilot-based desire for things to be different. When you are fully present with the moment, you may experience pain, but there will be no suffering.

This chapter has helped you explore how you think about yourself. The main message is that much of the suffering in life involves autopilot-based dissatisfaction with who we are. Now that you clearly understand that the mind is never satisfied for long, you know the solution is not to change yourself. Of course, this does not mean that you should stop trying to make self-improvements; if a change will make your life better, then by all means make the change. Rather, the point is that, no matter what you do or accomplish, there always will be some lingering sense of dissatisfaction. The fundamental problem of the mind's tendency to be dissatisfied needs a different approach. That approach is radical acceptance.

Radical Acceptance

The mindful approach is complete and total acceptance of your bipolar self as you are, today, in this very moment. It means being fully present with yourself and your life. It means experiencing at a deep level that, in each moment, the universe and everything in it—including you—is perfect as it is.

When sitting in meditation, Alex was able to experience the perfection of reality as it is. But at other times he wondered how everything could be perfect when there is so much suffering and unhappiness in the world. This is a question that many mindfulness practitioners ask. Are you deliberating about that too? Alex also questioned how he could be perfect when he had made so many mistakes in his life, some of which had hurt other people. Are you thinking about that as well? How can we simply accept all of this?

A mindful way to think about it is that reality already exists, whether we accept it or not. Our choice to accept it or not changes nothing. However, not accepting it, wanting things to be different, causes us to suffer. We can certainly want things to be different in the future, and try to change our situations so that they are. But we can't change right now, because it's already here.

You and the rest of reality are perfect in this moment, simply because you exist. You can experience this understanding through your mindfulness practice using the meditation that comes next.

Sitting with Yourself

The aim of this meditation is to help you deepen your mindfulness practice by asking the question, *Who is it that's watching your thoughts and emotions?* Read through the instructions and then do the meditation. A guided audio version of this meditation is also available online. Visit http://www.newharbinger.com/31854 to download it.

Getting ready: *Find a comfortable place where you won't be disturbed, as you have done for other sitting meditations. There is no other special preparation for this meditation. Just come as you are.*

Overview of the meditation: *Start with the sitting meditation focusing on the breath that you learned in chapter 4. First, sit with your attention focused on your breath. Then, expand your awareness to include all of the physical sensations in your body, including the breath. Finally, expand your awareness again to include the sounds around you, your thoughts, and your emotions. Now, look inward and ask yourself, Who is the watcher? Keep looking inward to see if you can see who is watching. Keep your attention on this question for about five minutes.*

Ending the meditation: *Bring the meditation to an end by focusing all of your attention on the breath for a minute or two.*

Spend a few minutes thinking about what you experienced. What did you learn about the nature of the watcher? Who is this awareness? You may discover that there is no watcher that you can identify. This might seem scary, but it is actually a pathway to freedom from suffering. Again, suffering is often tied to tightly held ideas and beliefs about ourselves as well as to our effort to be satisfied with who we are. Loosening our sense of self allows us greater freedom to experience ourselves and our lives simply as they are in each moment.

You may want to do this meditation several times each week as part of your regular practice.

Taking the Wider Perspective

As you have discovered in this chapter, mindfulness helps us loosen our hold on ideas and beliefs about ourselves. It helps us see the world with a less egocentric viewpoint. We can begin to see things from perspectives other than our own. This is incredibly liberating, and it opens us up to the world.

The ability to take in multiple perspectives can help you in relationships with others. You will form closer relationships when you can better appreciate where the other person is coming from. You will be more tolerant and forgiving of the imperfections of others as you see that they, like you, are often driven by autopilot. You will find more positives in your relationships and less conflict.

Finding Beginner's Mind

If you take away the thoughts, ideas, and beliefs that you have used to define youself, is anything left? You have looked inward to see who watches the thoughts and emotions and haven't found anyone there. So, what's left?

Awareness is left—awareness that is free of ideas and points of view. This is the awareness we experienced as infants, before language. In mindfulness terms, this is sometimes called *beginner's mind*, a mind that sees the world with wonder and awe, with curiosity and joy. This is being fully present with the moment. There are no philosophies, notions, or mind-sets between reality and you.

In mindfulness, you see that there is no need to define the awareness or figure out who you are. You don't need to accomplish anything or be satisfied or dissatisfied with yourself. All you have to do is just be, moment by moment and breath by breath.

In mindful awareness, the sense of self drops away. With this, the sense of being separate falls away too. You see that you are connected in a very real way to all living things. This powerful connection transforms your view of the world. You are not alone trying to survive. You are part of the vibrant cycle of life in a beautiful universe.

As your mindfulness practice deepens, you will become more comfortable with the selfless awareness of beginner's mind. You will find that you don't need to hold on to fixed beliefs about who you are or to ideas about who you should be. This, in and of itself, is truly liberating. You are free to be whoever you are in each moment. I invite you to relish that freedom and explore it.

Another benefit of shifting your perspective to a wider, less self-focused view is that you can see much more clearly that you are really not separate from the universe. This is the opposite of our habitual ego-based worldview, which some meditation traditions refer to as *small self*. From the small-self perspective, our autopilot-driven aim is to survive, and we tend to see the world in terms of whether a given person, place, or thing will help us or harm us. We often feel separate and disconnected from our planet and other living things. This small-self perspective is the reason that we spend much of our time feeling either fearful or full of desire. The brain is programmed to help us survive and thus tends to categorize our environment and what we experience in the world as either something to avoid, because it is dangerous, or something to desire that might benefit our survival. This programming has helped humans survive and prosper over the millennia, but it clearly does not enhance our psychological well-being in the modern world. Instead, it leaves us dissatisfied and anxious.

In contrast to this view, we can take a much more inclusive perspective that includes the entire universe. This is another way to understand selfless awareness. From this perspective, we can see that our small-self worldview is very limiting. We also can see that this worldview, along with autopilot, is the cause of our suffering.

From selfless awareness, we experience freedom from suffering. We are aware of pain, but there is space for it to arise and pass. And we can actually observe our small-self suffering, too, and feel compassion for him or her.

The perspective of selfless awareness leads to a deep and profound sense of being part of the universe, part of something much greater. There is no need to feel separate or afraid. Even our fear of death fades as we become less attached to the small-self viewpoint and feel more connected to the phenomena in the universe. Our own existence becomes less important.

All of this you must discover for yourself. In the end, mindfulness is an experiential practice. By that, I mean that, while it will be helpful to you to learn these concepts from reading this book, ultimately you have to decide for yourself whether what I say is true for you—based upon your own experience. Most practitioners of mindfulness experience states of selfless awareness and a sense of being part of something greater. For some, this occurs frequently, and for others, it may happen less often. The key is to be fully present with whatever you experience without preferring one experience over another.

More About Not Knowing

Earlier in the book, I introduced the concept of not knowing. By practicing mindfulness, we not only become more comfortable with the experience not knowing but we also realize just how much we don't know. We see that all ideas and concepts are at best only partial truths. We can't know everything about anything. In particular, we understand that we can't know everything about ourselves—about who we really are—because each moment is new. We are not the same person that we were ten years ago or ten minutes ago or even ten seconds ago.

On the one hand, not knowing can feel very scary. On the other hand, by fully experiencing this perspective, we can come to relax with it. We can see that we don't really need to know, after all. I hope you can discover this for yourself.

chapter 11

---

being bipolar
and happy

Mindfulness teaches us that suffering comes from what goes on in our heads, not from our circumstances or situations. Events and conditions may cause us pain, but suffering comes from autopilot, from our wanting things to be different from reality. In a more general way, autopilot keeps us from feeling joy, because it is never satisfied for long. Even when good things happen, our minds sometimes start wanting something else. So, you can see how our minds can cause us to be unhappy; but where do we find true happiness and joy?

This chapter will help you find happiness and joy in your bipolar life. To begin, it's important to clarify what true happiness is—and isn't.

Pleasure vs. Happiness

You might think that happiness is the feeling of pleasure you get by having a desire fulfilled. Your desire might be for a piece of cake or a new car or a college degree or anything. But the pleasure that you get from having your desire fulfilled is never true happiness, because the mind is never satisfied for long. Your sense of pleasure doesn't last, because your autopilot starts wanting something new. Also, many things that may give you pleasure are short-term experiences, like eating that piece of cake, so your sense of pleasure lasts only as long as the cake does.

To some degree, most of us confuse pleasure with happiness, and we seek pleasure as a way to be happy. There is nothing wrong with experiencing pleasure; and there is nothing wrong with seeking pleasure, as long as it doesn't cause harm to others or ourselves. But we need to see it for what it is—a short-term positive feeling, not the key to lasting happiness.

• Erin's Story

Erin has bipolar II disorder and has been a mindfulness practitioner for about five years. When she first started practicing, she found that mindfulness quickly helped her gain distance from her autopilot-based thoughts and emotions. Her life improved as she was able to avoid getting carried away with the ideas and feelings associated with mood episodes. Erin found that she suffered much less from her bipolar symptoms. However, she felt that happiness was still missing in her life.

By watching her thoughts over time, Erin was able to see that she was confusing pleasure with happiness. She realized that she was seeking pleasure when what she truly wanted was happiness. Mindfulness also taught her something else about pleasure, which is that if we watch our thoughts and emotions, we may find that we tend to cling to pleasure. We don't want to lose that good feeling. When it goes away, we may feel sadness or a sense of loss. From a mindfulness perspective, the aim is to experience pleasure fully but not cling to it. The point is to enjoy it and then let it go.

Erin discovered that pleasure was not the same as happiness, but she was still unclear about the true source of happiness, as many of us often are. Even if we know that pleasure is different from happiness, we still tend to believe that happiness comes from external conditions and situations, or good fortune. Erin thought that being in a committed long-term relationship would make her happy. After getting married, however, she realized that while she was more likely to feel happy than when she had been single, marriage wasn't a continuous state of bliss.

As Erin's mindfulness practice deepened, she was able to see that certain circumstances might be associated with her feeling happy, but these situations weren't the source of happiness.

Take a minute and ask yourself where happiness comes from. What ideas and beliefs do you have about what makes you happy?

Good Fortune vs. Happiness

Why aren't external situations the source of our joy? One reason is the fact that everything, including us, is impermanent. So, even if certain circumstances lead to good feelings, we can never be fully satisfied, because at some level we know the situation will have to end eventually. There is always some sense of fear that we'll lose the source of our happy condition. We may not be conscious of this most of the time, but it is there, giving us a vague sense of apprehension.

The other reason why external situations can't make us completely happy is that the mind is never satisfied for long. I keep coming back to this point because it is the central teaching of mindfulness. But please don't take my word for it.

Watch your own mind until you are convinced one way or the other. See for yourself how long your mind can stay satisfied and happy in response to situations, accomplishments, winning the lottery, or whatever.

Autopilot will lead you to believe that happiness is something you can get from somewhere. Are you beginning to see that this idea isn't true? Are you, like Erin, discovering that joy isn't out there somewhere for you to find?

Autopilot also may mislead you into thinking that happiness will happen at some time in the future. This is tied to the misconception that joy is something you can get from somewhere. We all have ideas that *I'll be happy when I graduate* or *when I retire* or *when my depression is better*...you get the picture.

The problem is that we can't inhabit the future. We can inhabit only the present moment. The only place happiness and joy can ever be found is right now.

Finding Beauty in the Moment

By being fully present with each moment, you can discover that you have been missing much of the beauty in life because your mind was somewhere else (on autopilot). Most of us are surprised to discover how much we were missing before we started practicing. Just being fully present with the things we like that are already occurring in our lives can be a game changer. Simply being present with the beauty in every moment is transformative. Look around you right now, and see if there isn't some beauty hiding right in front of your eyes.

Returning to Compassion

Compassion is a cornerstone of mindfulness practice as well as a key to finding happiness and joy. Without compassion, there can be no lasting gladness or satisfaction in life.

Erin discovered that one of her autopilot scripts was thinking that perhaps she didn't deserve to be happy because of mistakes she had made in her life. Some of these blunders had occurred as a result of mood episodes, and they caused her to experience lingering feelings of shame and guilt. It was helpful for Erin to see these painful autopilot scripts as lacking in substance. Then, going further in her practice, she was able to develop a profound sense of compassion for herself, which allowed her to forgive herself for past misjudgments and to embrace the idea that she deserved to be happy.

Do you have any similar habitual thinking patterns that may be keeping you from feeling happy? Can you work on becoming more compassionate toward yourself?

Compassion for ourselves is a key to happiness, but equally important is developing a deep and abiding concern for others. One reason is that compassion helps us forgive the imperfections of those we care about. It helps us see that, like us, everyone is driven by autopilot. We can become more tolerant as we recognize this fact. Compassion for other living beings also helps us find the pathway to lasting joy.

Compassion arises from selfless awareness. As discussed in chapter 10, by letting go of our tight grasp on our ideas and beliefs about ourselves, we take on a wider and more open viewpoint, in which we see ourselves more as part of the universe than as separate beings. From that perspective, we see that harm to others is harm to us and that damage to our selves is damage to the universe. Thus, we naturally experience compassion for all living things, including our small self.

From Compassion, Love Arises

Just as our minds fool us about the nature of happiness, our autopilot misleads us about love. Like happiness, we think that love is something we can get, or acquire. While it is true that we can be loved, we can't get a bucket of love from someone that we can carry around with us. This misunderstanding leads to disappointment. Ultimately, while being loved is important, our confusion about what love is can make the actual experience disappointing.

Mindfulness teaches us that the kind of love that makes us most happy is the love that we feel toward others. To put it another way, love is something that we give, not something that we collect.

By seeing the true nature of the mind, compassion arises. From compassion, love for ourselves and others develops. Giving love makes us happy.

Appreciating Bipolar as a Gift

Mindfulness can teach you to view your illness as a gift. Does that sound ridiculous? It seemed ridiculous to Erin, at first. But over time, as she practiced mindfulness, she realized that having to live with such a challenging illness actually enhanced her ability to feel compassion and love for others. Surprisingly, Erin found that her bipolar disorder helped her experience the joy of caring.

At another level, Erin came to realize that the pathway to liberation from suffering was through being fully present with life, including all of the pain. Bipolar disorder forced her to experience painful emotional states over and over again. On the one hand, this was incredibly difficult. On the other hand, it was a direct pathway to her being able to be fully present with whatever life had to offer.

Once more, mindfulness is about shifting perspective. Can you make the same shift in perspective that Erin made? Can you see your illness as an expressway to freedom from suffering? Can you see it as a source of love and compassion in your life?

Finding Happiness and Joy

Now you know that happiness isn't something that you can get from anyone or anything. You also know that feeling compassion for, and giving love to, yourself and others plays a role in your ability to experience joy. But knowing these things still doesn't tell you where to find joy and happiness.

So, where do you look? The answer is, of course, in the present moment. Happiness is always available to you right here and right now. It's not a matter of finding it somewhere else. You can't get it, because you already have it. It's been with you all along, but you just couldn't see it. Your autopilot thinking was in the way. From the viewpoint of mindful awareness, you can be happy and joyful in this very moment—and in the next moment, and in the one after that. That's the gift of mindfulness.

Sitting with Joy

This meditation will help you experience the happiness and joy that already exist in every moment. Read through the instructions and then do the meditation. A guided audio version of this meditation is also available online: visit http://www.newharbin ger.com/31854 to access it.

Getting started: *Find a comfortable place to sit where you won't be disturbed. You don't need any other special preparation for this meditation.*

Overview of the meditation: *Start with the sitting meditation focusing on the breath that you learned in chapter 4. First, focus attention on your breath. Then expand your awareness to include all of the physical sensations in your body, including the breath. Finally, expand your awareness again to include sounds, thoughts, and emotions. Now allow happiness and joy to arise. Sit with the positive feelings (and any others that come up) for about five minutes.*

Ending the meditation: *End the meditation by focusing all of your attention on the breath for a minute or two.*

Afterward, spend a few minutes thinking about what you learned from this meditation. Did you experience positive feelings? If so, how did your body feel during that time? What thoughts were passing through your head?

You may not always find that happiness and joy arise when you practice this meditation. Sometimes autopilot may be preventing you from experiencing these feelings. That's okay. In fact, it's actually good, because it allows you to practice with whatever thinking patterns may be keeping you from feeling happiness and joy. Ultimately, recognizing these thinking ruts and moving out of them into mindful awareness will strengthen your practice and enhance your ability to experience joy in the moment.

Practice this meditation several times each week as part of your regular practice.

Mindfulness as a Spiritual Practice

Mindfulness was developed as a secular practice from Buddhist spiritual traditions. It can be totally nonspiritual, it can be spiritual in practice, or it can be a mix of both. While this book has not mentioned spirituality before this, spirituality can be defined in many ways, and I like to think of it as anything that involves personal transformation and growth. Using that definition, then, this book has been all about a spiritual practice. With that in mind, you may want a certain spiritual component to your mindfulness practice.

Most spiritual and religious traditions have a strong focus on kindness and compassion toward others, which, I believe, is the ultimate source of happiness. Chapter 10 explored how mindfulness can lead you to loosen your clinging to a sense of self so that you can experience an awareness that has a strong connection with all living things. In this chapter, you further discovered that out of such selfless awareness, compassion and love arise. Compassion and love serve as the foundation of happiness, and directing compassion and love toward others will magnify your joy.

I encourage you to incorporate helping other living beings into your mindfulness practice. Bipolar disorder gives you a great understanding of suffering, which you can use to help others. There are many ways that you might do this. As you know, the world is full of need. Find what resonates with you. Choose something that you are passionate about. Experience unlimited happiness by giving love and helping others.

Living Mindfully with Bipolar Disorder

Congratulations on finishing this book and for developing your personal mindfulness practice! As a result of your efforts, you can now live better with bipolar disorder.

Please keep your mindfulness practice going. This can be challenging for all of us. Life tends to get in the way, and it can be difficult to find time to practice. I encourage you to make your practice one of the top priorities in your life.

Again, many of us find that practicing with a group is very helpful. Consider doing a web search for local meditation groups that you might be able to join. Take a live mindfulness class if you haven't done so and if one is available where you live. Look for resources on the Internet. You are invited to connect with other practitioners by joining my online mindfulness community at http://www.WilliamR MarchandMD.com.

It has been my pleasure to serve as your guide through this process. Writing this has been part of my personal mindfulness practice, and it is an honor and a privilege to practice with you.

appendix

---

more options for your mindfulness practice

This appendix includes several more meditations that you can use in your daily practice. It ends with a description of how to sit in Burmese meditation posture.

There are many different meditations that you can use in your mindfulness practice. I encourage you to experiment to find several that you like and look forward to doing on a daily basis. Here are some that you may want to try.

Compassion Meditation

One goal of a mindfulness practice is to develop a deep sense of caring and compassion, first for ourselves and then for others. Compassion meditations are also known as loving-kindness meditations.

In compassion meditations, you use a *mantra*, which is a phrase that you repeat during meditation. It can be used as an anchor for concentration, as you use the breath. In this case, you use the mantra to keep your focus on compassion. You might want to start with this: "May I be happy. May I be healthy. May I have peace."

Start the meditation by focusing on the breath for a few minutes. Then just repeat your mantra over and over to yourself, keeping your attention on the words. If you want, you can experiment with different wording.

To develop compassion for others, try this as a mantra: "May we be happy. May we be healthy. May we have peace." The "we" here can be a specific group of people (your family, your meditation group) or people in general. You also can use a specific person's name instead of saying "we." A guided audio version of this meditation is available online: visit http://www.newharbinger .com/31854 to access it, or see the very end of this book for more information.

Movement and Activity Meditations

Any activity that you do with mindful awareness can be a meditation. The meditations in this section can help you live mindfully by incorporating mindful awareness into your daily life.

Mindful Activities

Try doing your everyday activities with mindful awareness. Brushing your teeth, taking out the garbage, and cleaning the bathroom may not be your favorite things to do, but you can do them with full awareness of the moment rather than with your mind on autopilot. Try doing one activity mindfully every time you do it for a week. You could try eating one meal mindfully each week. As you start practicing mindfulness every day, you may discover that you have been missing much of life because your mind has been on autopilot.

Walking Meditations

Walking is a great activity to do mindfully. Any time that you walk, you can choose to walk mindfully. This is being fully present with the moment, being aware of sights, sounds, and physical sensations as they occur. You may find it helpful to pay particular attention to the physical sensations of moving your body. As always, when your mind goes on autopilot, gently direct your attention back to the present moment.

In addition to walking mindfully—which you can do anytime you feel like it—you can make a walking meditation one of your daily practices. This is a great way to add variety to your practice. Some people use walking meditation as their primary daily form of practice. You can do a walking meditation by walking in a park, on a hike, or even walking on the street. It is important to set the intention that the walk is for the purpose of meditation. As with mindful walking, keep your attention focused on the present moment. Try not to cling to sights or sounds, but let them just arise and pass. When the mind wanders on autopilot, just notice it happening. Let the thoughts come and go in the background while keeping your attention on what is happening right now.

Another way to do walking meditation is to walk slowly. This can work well for an indoor walking meditation. Try walking in half steps, moving your foot a half step with each complete breath. You move your right foot forward one half step with one inhalation and exhalation, and then move your left foot forward one half step with the next inhalation and exhalation, and so on.

Sitting Meditation with Open Awareness

This is an advanced meditation sometimes called *open monitoring*. In it, rather than keeping your attention on an anchor such as the breath, you sit in open awareness, observing phenomena arise and pass. This is an important meditation for your practice, because in open awareness you can clearly see that thoughts and emotions are like all other phenomena (sights, sounds, and sensations). They come and go and have no special meaning.

Start this meditation with focus on the breath, and then move to open awareness. A guided audio version of this meditation that will guide you through the steps is available online. Visit http://www.newharbinger.com/31854 to access it, or see the very end of this book for more information.

Burmese Meditation Posture

It is perfectly fine to do all your sitting meditations in a chair. However, the Burmese posture is a good alternative that you might want to try. You sit with Burmese posture on cushions on the floor as shown in figure 4.1.

To sit Burmese pose, it is best to have cushions especially made for sitting meditation: a zafu (the round cushion) and a zabuton (the thick mat on which the zafu rests). You can get these cushions at any store that sells meditation supplies.

In Burmese position, your bottom is on the zafu and you cross one leg in front of the other on the zabuton. The idea is that your bottom and knees form a tripod that supports the rest of you. Thus, it is critical to have both knees resting on the zabuton. You may have to adjust the height of the zafu to get both knees onto the zabuton. To accomplish this, some people need to use more than one zafu or add thin pads under each knee.

Start by settling on the zafu. It can be helpful to rock gently from side to side to find a stable position. Next, tilt your pelvis forward so that your belly sticks out a bit. Now extend your spine up. You want to be sitting so that your body is hanging off of your spine, which is supported by the tripod formed by your bottom and your knees. Your head should be directly over your shoulders, not tilted forward or back. Tuck your chin slightly. Rest your left hand on your lap and then put your right hand on top of the left—the back of the right hand is resting on the palm of the left. Your thumbs should be horizontal with the end of one thumb just touching the end of the other.

Now you are in Burmese pose. From here, you can do any of the sitting meditations in this book.

glossary

Amygdala: Brain structure located in the temporal lobes (one on each side) that functions as a threat detector and warning system. Contributes to the anxiety of bipolar disorder.

Autopilot: The mindfulness term for the way the mind normally works, which is focused on the past and future rather than the present moment.

Axon: Section of the neuron that carries an electrical signal to the synapse.

Bipolar disorder: An illness characterized by episodes of feeling down and depressed as well as periods of elevated mood (mania or hypomania).

Bipolar spectrum: The group of related bipolar disorders—bipolar I, bipolar II, and cyclothymia—as well as unspecified bipolar disorders and bipolar disorders from medical conditions.

Dendrites: Regions of the neuron that receive signals from other neurons.

Euthymic: Mood at baseline, neither depressed nor elevated.

Hypomania: Milder mood elevation that does not meet the full criteria for a manic episode.

Mania: Severe episode of mood elevation that results in significant impairment and/or psychosis and/or hospitalization.

Mindfulness: A meditation-based practice with the aim of keeping awareness focused on sights, sounds, thoughts, and emotions as they occur in the present moment.

Neural circuit: A group of connected neurons that work together. Also called a neural network.

Neuron: A nerve cell. Transmits information from one place to another in the nervous system.

Neuroplasticity: The capacity of the brain to change in response to the environment. The brain can rewire itself in response to mindfulness training.

Neurotransmitter: Chemical that transmits information from one neuron to another at the synapse. Abnormalities of neurotransmitter function contribute to symptoms of bipolar disorder.

Synapse: Brain structure that allows transmission of information from one neuron to another.

suggested reading

Calming Your Anxious Mind: How Mindfulness and Compassion Can Free You from Anxiety, Fear, and Panic, second edition, by Jeffrey Brantley and Jon Kabat-Zinn. Oakland, CA: New Harbinger Publications, 2007.

Depression and Bipolar Disorder: Your Guide to Recovery, by William R. Marchand. Boulder, CO: Bull Publishing Company, 2012.

Full Catastrophe Living: Using the Wisdom of Your Body and Mind to Face Stress, Pain, and Illness, revised edition, by Jon Kabat-Zinn. New York: Bantam Books, 2013.

Healing the Angry Brain: How Understanding the Way Your Brain Works Can Help You Control Anger and Aggression, by Ronald Potter-Efron. Oakland, CA: New Harbinger Publications, 2012.

A Mindfulness-Based Stress Reduction Workbook, by Bob Stahl and Elisha Goldstein. Oakland, CA: New Harbinger Publications, 2010.

The Mindful Way Through Depression: Freeing Yourself from Chronic Unhappiness, by Mark Williams, John Teasdale, Zindel Segal, and Jon Kabat-Zinn. New York: Guilford Press, 2007.

The Tao of Bipolar: Using Meditation and Mindfulness to Find Balance and Peace, by C. Alexander Simpkins and Annellen M. Simpkins. Oakland, CA: New Harbinger Publications, 2013.

references

American Psychiatric Association. 2013. *Diagnostic and Statistical Manual of Mental Disorders (DSM-5)*. 5th ed. Arlington, VA: American Psychiatric Association.

Campbell, T. S., L. E. Labelle, S. L. Bacon, P. Faris, and L. E. Carlson. 2012. "Impact of Mindfulness-Based Stress Reduction (MBSR) on Attention, Rumination and Resting Blood Pressure in Women with Cancer: A Waitlist-Controlled Study." *Journal of Behavioral Medicine* 35 (3): 262–71.

Chadwick, P., H. Kaur, M. Swelam, S. Ross, and L. Ellett. 2011. "Experience of Mindfulness in People with Bipolar Disorder: A Qualitative Study." *Psychotherapy Research: Journal of the Society for Psychotherapy Research* 21 (3): 277–85.

Deckersbach, T., B. K. Holzel, L. R. Eisner, J. P. Stange, A. D. Peckham, D. D. Dougherty, S. L. Rauch, S. Lazar, and A. A. Nierenberg. 2012. "Mindfulness-Based Cognitive Therapy for Nonremitted Patients with Bipolar Disorder." *CNS Neuroscience and Therapeutics* 18 (2): 133–41.

Goldin, P. R., and J. J. Gross. 2010. "Effects of Mindfulness-Based Stress Reduction (MBSR) on Emotion Regulation in Social Anxiety Disorder." *Emotion* 10 (1): 83–91.

Goodwin, G. M. 2009. "Evidence-Based Guidelines for Treating Bipolar Disorder: Revised Second Edition— Recommendations from the British Association for Psychopharmacology." *Journal of Psychopharmacology* 23 (4): 346–88.

Grunze, H., E. Vieta, G. M. Goodwin, C. Bowden, R. W. Licht, H. J. Moller, and S. Kasper. 2010. "The World Federation of Societies of Biological Psychiatry (WFSBP) Guidelines for the Biological Treatment of Bipolar Disorders: Update 2010 on the Treatment of Acute Bipolar Depression." *World Journal of Biological Psychiatry* 11 (2): 81–109.

Ives-Deliperi, V. L., F. Howells, D. J. Stein, E. M. Meintjes, and N. Horn. 2013. "The Effects of Mindfulness-Based Cognitive Therapy in Patients with Bipolar Disorder: A Controlled Functional MRI Investigation." *Journal of Affective Disorders* 150 (3): 1152–57.

Kabat-Zinn, J. 2013. *Full Catastrophe Living: Using the Wisdom of Your Body and Mind to Face Stress, Pain, and Illness.* Rev. ed. New York: Bantam Books.

Miklowitz, D. J. 2008. "Adjunctive Psychotherapy for Bipolar Disorder: State of the Evidence." *The American Journal of Psychiatry* 165 (11): 1408–19.

Nivoli, A. M., F. Colom, A. Murru, I. Pacchiarotti, P. Castro-Loli, A. Gonzalez-Pinto, K. N. Fountoulakis, and E. Vieta. 2011. "New Treatment Guidelines for Acute Bipolar Depression: A Systematic Review." *Journal of Affective Disorders* 129 (1–3): 14–26.

Pacchiarotti, I., M. Valenti, F. Colom, A. R. Rosa, A. M. Nivoli, A. Murru, J. Sanchez-Moreno, and E. Vieta. 2011. "Differential Outcome of Bipolar Patients Receiving Antidepressant Monotherapy Versus Combination with an Antimanic Drug." *Journal of Affective Disorders* 129 (1–3): 321–26.

Perich, T., V. Manicavasagar, P. B. Mitchell, J. R. Ball, and D. Hadzi-Pavlovic. 2013. "A Randomized Controlled Trial of Mindfulness-Based Cognitive Therapy for Bipolar Disorder." *Acta Psychiatrica Scandinavica* 127 (5): 333–43.

Scherk, H., F. G. Pajonk, and S. Leucht. 2007. "Second-Generation Antipsychotic Agents in the Treatment of Acute Mania: A Systematic Review and Meta-Analysis of Randomized Controlled Trials." *Archives of General Psychiatry* 64 (4): 442–55.

Segal, Z. V., P. Bieling, T. Young, G. MacQueen, R. Cooke, L. Martin, R. Bloch, and R. D. Levitan. 2010. "Antidepressant Monotherapy vs. Sequential Pharmaco-therapy and Mindfulness-Based Cognitive Therapy, or Placebo, for Relapse Prophylaxis in Recurrent Depression." *Archives of General Psychiatry* 67 (12): 1256–64.

Segal, Z. V., J. M. G. Williams, and J. D. Teasdale. 2002. *Mindfulness-Based Cognitive Therapy for Depression: A New Approach to Preventing Relapse.* New York: Guilford Press.

Sienaert, P., L. Lambrichts, A. Dols, and J. De Fruyt. 2013. "Evidence-Based Treatment Strategies for Treatment-Resistant Bipolar Depression: A Systematic Review." *Bipolar Disorders* 15 (1): 61–69.

Van Aalderen, J. R., A. R. Donders, F. Giommi, P. Spinhoven, H. P. Barendregt, and A. E. Speckens. 2012. "The Efficacy of Mindfulness-Based Cognitive Therapy in Recurrent Depressed Patients with and without a Current Depressive Episode: A Randomized Controlled Trial." *Psychological Medicine* 42 (5): 989–1001.

Vazquez, G., L. Tondo, and R. J. Baldessarini. 2011. "Comparison of Antidepressant Responses in Patients with Bipolar vs. Unipolar Depression: A Meta-Analytic Review." *Pharmacopsychiatry* 44 (1): 21–26.

Vollestad, J., B. Sivertsen, and G. H. Nielsen. 2011. "Mindfulness-Based Stress Reduction for Patients with Anxiety Disorders: Evaluation in a Randomized Controlled Trial." *Behavioral Research and Therapy* 49 (4): 281–88.

Weber, B., F. Jermann, M. Gex-Fabry, A. Nallet, G. Bondolfi, and J. M. Aubry. 2010. "Mindfulness-Based Cognitive Therapy for Bipolar Disorder: A Feasibility Trial." *European Psychiatry: The Journal of the Association of European Psychiatrists* 25 (6): 334–37.

Yatham, L. N., S. H. Kennedy, A. Schaffer, S. V. Parikh, S. Beaulieu, C. O'Donovan, G. MacQueen, R. S. McIntyre, V. Sharma, A. Ravindran, L. T. Young, A. H. Young, M. Alda, R. Milev, E. Vieta, J. R. Calabrese, M. Berk, K. Ha, and F. Kapczinski. 2009. "Canadian Network for Mood and Anxiety Treatments (CANMAT) and International Society for Bipolar Disorders (ISBD) Collaborative Update of CANMAT Guidelines for the Management of Patients with Bipolar Disorder: Update 2009." *Bipolar Disorders* 11 (3): 225–55.5

William R. Marchand, MD, is a mindfulness teacher, board-certified psychiatrist and neuroscientist, clinical associate professor of psychiatry, and adjunct assistant professor of psychology at the University of Utah. Additionally, he is the Associate Chief of Mental Health and Chief of Psychiatry at the George. E. Wahlen Department of Veterans Affairs Medical Center. He has years of experience treating bipolar disorder, researching the neurobiology of mood and anxiety disorders, and teaching mindfulness. His personal mindfulness practice is in the Soto Zen tradition, in which he is an ordained monk. He lives in Salt Lake City, UT.

FROM OUR PUBLISHER—

As the publisher at New Harbinger and a clinical psychologist since 1978, I know that emotional problems are best helped with evidence-based therapies. These are the treatments derived from scientific research (randomized controlled trials) that show what works. Whether these treatments are delivered by trained clinicians or found in a self-help book, they are designed to provide you with proven strategies to overcome your problem.

Therapies that aren't evidence-based—whether offered by clinicians or in books—are much less likely to help. In fact, therapies that aren't guided by science may not help you at all. That's why this New Harbinger book is based on scientific evidence that the treatment can relieve emotional pain.

This is important: if this book isn't enough, and you need the help of a skilled therapist, use the following resources to find a clinician trained in the evidence-based protocols appropriate for your problem. And if you need more support—a community that understands what you're going through and can show you ways to cope—resources for that are provided below, as well.

Real help is available for the problems you have been struggling with. The skills you can learn from evidence-based therapies will change your life.

Matthew McKay, PhD
Publisher, New Harbinger Publications